ULYSSES
S.GRANT

LEADERSHIP ▪ STRATEGY ▪ CONFLICT

MARK LARDAS ▪ ILLUSTRATED BY ADAM HOOK

First published in 2012 by Osprey Publishing
Midland House, West Way, Botley, Oxford OX2 0PH, UK
44-02 23rd St, Suite 219, Long Island City, NY 11101, USA

E-mail: info@ospreypublishing.com

Print ISBN: 978 1 84908 733 9
PDF e-book ISBN: 978 1 849087 346
EPUB e-book ISBN: 978 1 780961 170

Editorial by Ilios Publishing Ltd, Oxford, UK (www.iliospublishing.com)
Cartography: Mapping Specialists Ltd.
Page layout by The Black Spot
Index by Marie-Pierre Evans
Originated by PDQ Media, Bungay, UK
Printed in China through Worldprint Ltd.

12 13 14 15 16 10 9 8 7 6 5 4 3 2 1

Dedication
This book is dedicated to my son William, who is turning out to be a leader.

Author's note
USAHI – United States Army Historical Institute
LOC – Library of Congress, Washington, DC
AC – Author's Collection

Artist's note
Readers may care to note that the original paintings from which the colour plates in this book were prepared are available for private sale. All reproduction copyright whatsoever is retained by the Publishers. All enquiries should be addressed to:

Scorpio Gallery, 158 Mill Road, Hailsham, East Sussex, BN27 2SH, UK
E-mail: scorpiopaintings@btinternet.com

The Publishers regret that they can enter into no correspondence upon this matter.

[front-cover image credit]
Library of Congress

The Woodland Trust
Osprey Publishing are supporting the Woodland Trust, the UK's leading woodland conservation charity, by funding the dedication of trees.

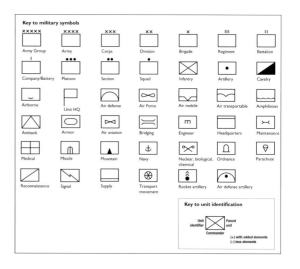

CONTENTS

INTRODUCTION

Ulysses Grant had many names during his lifetime. He was born Hiram Ulysses Grant. When he went to West Point, his nomination called him "Ulysses S. Grant," which thereafter became his legal name as the Army refused to correct the error. At West Point and during his subsequent career in the Regular Army, his fellow cadets and officers called him "Sam Grant" – after all, U. S. stood for Uncle Sam. After being forced to resign his commission and failing at every business he attempted, his neighbors in Galena, Illinois called him "Useless" Grant. Everyone wrote Grant off as a loser.

Grant earned the nickname "Unconditional Surrender" Grant following the delivery of this note, reproduced in facsimile, to the commander of Fort Donelson, stating "no terms except an unconditional and immediate surrender can be accepted." (AC)

Then the Civil War began and Grant acquired several new names. Because he had military experience – he had gone to West Point and served in the Regular Army as an officer – he became Colonel Grant in an Illinois volunteer regiment when he enlisted in the Army. Through sheer competence – and overcoming a bad reputation – he quickly became Brigadier-General and then Major-General Grant. After he led the first successful major Union offensive of the war – which resulted in the capture of Forts Henry and Donelson – "Useless" Grant disappeared, to be replaced by "Unconditional Surrender" Grant. It turned out "Useless Grant" had a talent it took a war to reveal – he won battles.

Forts Henry and Donelson proved not to be flukes. Grant would continue winning victories with a consistency unmatched by any other general in the American Civil War – on either side of the conflict.

Despite – or perhaps because of – his ability to win battles, Grant had as many enemies among the officer corps of the Union Army as he had in the Confederate Army. Henry Halleck, Grant's immediate superior in the first years of the Civil

War, was reluctant to trust Grant in an independent command, despite Grant's ability to win battles when acting independently.

When it appeared that Grant would be relieved after Shiloh, President Lincoln, Grant's biggest supporter, scotched this attempt. "I can't spare this man," Lincoln said of Grant. "He fights." When fellow generals claimed he was drinking again, Lincoln is reputed to have replied, "Find out what he drinks, and send my other commanders a case!"

Grant was a lightning rod for criticism. He did drink to excess at times. His resignation from the army in 1854 had been occasioned by accusations of drinking on duty. The evidence as to whether the accusation was accurate is murky. After the fall of Vicksburg, however, Grant went on a monumental drinking spree that would have cost

him his career if it had occurred earlier. He went on a bender after a failed assault at Cold Harbor. On the other hand, despite accusations, Grant was never drunk before or during a battle.

Grant did not match the popular image of a general. His opponent Robert E. Lee was tall, immaculately turned out, and formidably formal. Grant was short and rumpled – an unimposing figure. More than once in his military career, superior officers instructed Grant to improve his appearance. Throughout the Civil War Grant dressed simply. He often wore a private's tunic embellished with epaulets marking his general's rank rather than the elaborate uniforms favored by his colleagues and opponents.

Grant was also criticized as a poor commander. Many claimed that Grant was simply a butcher. He often won in an ugly manner. At Shiloh, a disastrous first day was followed with a powerful counterattack that swept the Confederates from the field. Vicksburg required several attempts – the first of which was repulsed – but in the end, Vicksburg yielded to Grant. When he moved east and attached himself to the Army of the Potomac he faced the Confederacy's greatest general – Robert E. Lee. Grant and Lee fought a series of battles that caused the Confederacy's strategic position to deteriorate with each battle, even though at each Lee achieved what should have been a victory on a tactical level.

Yet Grant did win and was one of the few Union generals that did so consistently. Most of the others that won consistently were his protégés, such as William T. Sherman, Philip Sheridan, and James B. McPherson. Other generals, such as Joseph Hooker and George Thomas, performed better after serving under Grant.

Victory had its rewards. In March 1864 Grant became Lieutenant-General Grant, the only United States Army officer except for George Washington and Winfield Scott to achieve that rank. After the war Grant would become the United States Army's first full general. Soon after that the United States awarded him another name – President Ulysses S. Grant.

At Appomattox, when Robert E. Lee surrendered the Army of Northern Virginia, Grant departed from the reputation of "Unconditional Surrender" Grant, allowing surrender terms that made it impossible to punish Confederate soldiers for fighting against the United States. (USAHI)

In a very real sense, winning battles was one of the few things Grant did right. Not only was his life a failure before the Civil War, but much of his life after the Civil War was a failure, too. Elected president by a grateful nation, the Grant presidency was scarred by corruption scandals and an economic panic. While Grant was personally honest, he chose his cabinet poorly, relying on his wartime experience with the individual rather than the individual's integrity to guide his judgment. Neither Grant's prewar business experience – all the businesses he tried failed – nor his Civil War military experience provided him with the understanding to deal with the national economy. After he left the presidency more bad business judgments – including trusting the wrong people – left him bankrupt.

Yet Grant's major talent – winning battles – earns him a place among America's great men. He was the country's greatest general since George Washington. And like Washington, Grant's battlefield performance was the only factor standing between the United States continuing as one, indivisible nation. Grant was the keystone of the Union victory, a man whose removal would have resulted in the Union cause crumbling into defeat – and the United States dissolving into a collection of competing sovereign states. The only generals that could have replaced Grant were those developed by him, generals that would not have been in a position to replace him until Grant had the Civil War won.

THE EARLY YEARS

Hiram Ulysses Grant was born on April 27, 1822, at Point Pleasant in Clermont County, Ohio. He was the oldest of six children – three boys and three girls – born to Jesse Root Grant and Hannah Grant (née Simpson). In many ways he was indistinguishable from the tens of thousands of others born near the American frontier in the 1820s and 1830s. Both parents came from families that had been in North America for generations. His father's family came to the New World in the 1630s, and his mother's family settled in Pennsylvania early in the 18th century.

His family, while respected locally, was solidly rooted in the yeoman stock of the era. His father, Jesse Root Grant was a tanner. Despite only a rudimentary education, he was noted for his scholarship,

Grant's birthplace was an unremarkable frame house in southern Ohio. Grant came from a family that had been in the United States for generations, and prospered through hard work. (LOC)

achieved largely though independent and voracious reading. His mother was a modest woman whom her son described as, "unselfish, devoted to her family, thoroughly good, conscientious, intelligent, never meddling with other person's affairs, genuinely pious without any cant, with a strong sense of right and justice; unobtrusive, kindhearted, and attached to her church and country."

His father had learned the tanning trade under Owen Brown, a Deerfield Ohio tanner who moved to Point Pleasant in 1819 to serve as foreman for a tannery. In 1832 Jesse Grant bought land in Georgetown, Ohio, and moved his family there, running his own tannery, farm, and woodlot.

Growing up in rural America, Hiram Ulysses was an unremarkable child. He worked at his father's tannery (which he detested), helped harvest timber on the woodlot, and plowed the farm (activities he enjoyed). He proved skilled with horses, but an indifferent scholar. His poor school performance probably had less to do with a lack of intelligence than it did with boredom. The local county schools he attended did not challenge him. In Grant's words, "the highest branches taught [were]—the three R's, 'Reading, 'Riting, 'Rithmetic.' I never saw an algebra, or other mathematical work higher than the arithmetic, in Georgetown, until after I was appointed to West Point."

Jesse Grant sent the boy to boarding schools during the winters of 1836–37 and 1838–39, but as all these institutions taught were the lessons he had already learned at the subscription school in Georgetown, he remained an indifferent student. His schoolmates dubbed him "Useless Grant." Knowing his son did not intend to take over the tannery, and recognizing something in him that others missed, Jesse Grant wanted Hiram to attend college for a chance at life as something other than a farmer, but the family lacked the funds for tuition and board.

Jesse Grant had political connections, however. He had been a regular contributor to Ohio newspapers and was prominent in Whig politics in Ohio. Unknown to Hiram Ulysses, his father had asked Senator Thomas Morris to appoint the boy to the United States Military Academy at West Point. Morris did so, getting Grant's Representative to nominate Jesse Grant's son.

THE MILITARY LIFE

Hiram was initially unimpressed with the appointment. When told of the unsought appointment his immediate reaction was to tell his father, "But I won't go." In his memoirs Grant claimed that his initial opposition to attending West Point was due to a fear of failure. This after-the-fact explanation was probably a result of his later experiences, especially those between leaving the Army in 1854 and the Civil War, when he succeeded at nothing. The boy had no real objections other than the distance involved, and the fact that he had not been informed previously. Nor had he sought a military career or further education.

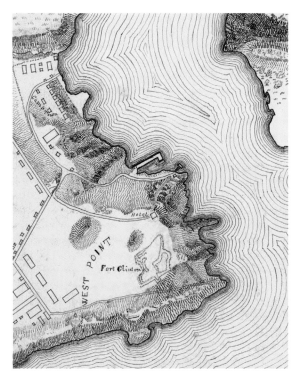

West Point was the United States' first engineering college. In 1843, when this map of West Point was created, it was one of the finest colleges in the country, and one of the few places where a college education could be obtained without paying tuition. (LOC)

The United States Military Academy had been established by Congress in 1802 to train officers for the United States Army. Initially there had been considerable opposition to the institution, as many in the Jeffersonian and Jacksonian eras of United States' history feared its graduates would create an elitist, European-style aristocracy in the new republic. A bill abolishing the Academy had been introduced as late as 1839, Grant's first year at West Point.

Although the school got off to a rocky start, Sylvanus Thayer, who was appointed Superintendent in 1817 and ran the Military Academy until 1833, transformed it into one of the republic's finest educational institutions. Civil engineering formed the core of the Academy's curriculum. Until 1824, it was the only engineering school in the United States. By the time Grant arrived in the summer of 1839, most of the nation's formally trained engineers were West Point graduates. The education was free – and graduates were commissioned as officers in the United States Army, with the prestige associated with a status that presumably made a man a gentleman.

Through a misunderstanding on the part of the Representative making Grant's appointment, his name was recorded as Ulysses Simpson Grant, not Hiram Ulysses Grant and Grant's subsequent attempts to correct the error failed before an unyielding Army bureaucracy. The cadet appointed to the Military Academy was listed as Ulysses Simpson Grant. He could call himself whatever he wished off-duty, but while on duty Ulysses Simpson Grant it would remain.

Ulysses S. Grant proved a lackluster cadet during his four years at West Point. While he had easily passed his entrance examination, he had not sought out a career in the military. However, West Point held some attractions. It had an excellent library, and Grant devoted considerable amounts of time to reading – although, by his own admission, he spent more time reading novels than textbooks. He also showed an interest in and an aptitude for mathematics. One reason that he stuck with the Academy was because he hoped to become an assistant professor of mathematics there after graduation, and then find a permanent position as professor at a civilian college upon fulfilling his military obligations.

He was popular with his fellow cadets, and soon gained the nickname "Sam" Grant, from his initials. U. S. Grant became "Uncle Sam" Grant, which was soon shortened to Sam Grant. He also proved an excellent horseman. Poor academic performance in French, tactics, and, especially, conduct dragged down his standing. Upon graduation, in 1843, Grant was in the bottom half of his graduating class, although just barely – 21st in a class of 39.

Although in the middle of his class, his years at West Point gave Grant a solid professional grounding. He would have mastered the basics of running a military unit as large as a regiment, then the largest permanent formation maintained by the United States Army. He would also have understood the strengths and limitations of the standard weapons of the day.

If a West Point education had one weakness it was in the tactics and strategy then taught, which were drawn from the experience of the French Revolutionary and Napoleonic Wars, already a generation past. Changes in weapons technology – most notably the rifled musket and contact-fused shell – meant that the old tactics had been superseded. In many ways, Napoleonic-era tactics were as relevant to the American Civil War battle as World War II tactics were to the 1991 Gulf War.

Ulysses Grant was a solid, but unremarkable cadet at West Point, graduating in the middle of his class. While he disliked the regimentation, his ambition upon graduation was to return as a professor. (LOC)

Because of his horsemanship, and aptitude with horses, Grant would have been an outstanding cavalryman. He applied for a commission in the cavalry, with his second choice a posting in the 4th Infantry Regiment. The United States Army in 1843 had only one cavalry regiment, and appointments were filled by class standing. The most sought-after postings were in engineering, cavalry and artillery, and those in the upper half of the graduating class quickly filled these openings. On September 30, 1843, 2nd Lieutenant Sam Grant reported for duty with the 4th Infantry, then at Jefferson Barracks, St. Louis, Missouri.

He was not to remain long at Jefferson Barracks. Within six months his regiment was ordered to Louisiana, to form part of the Army of Observation watching over events in Texas. Then an independent republic, Texas was in negotiation with the United States for admission to the Union. As Mexico was expected to oppose annexation of territory it claimed as part of Mexico, the United States government was moving troops to intervene in Texas if necessary.

The brief stay at St. Louis had an important impact on Grant's future, however. The family of his friend and West Point roommate, Frederick T. Dent, lived close to Jefferson Barracks. Grant was a frequent visitor to the Dent household, where he became acquainted with Dent's sister, Julia. The couple soon fell in love. They would marry in 1848, the nuptials delayed by war with Mexico, and Grant's service during that conflict.

The upcoming war also derailed Grant's attempt to enter the professorate. While at Jefferson Barracks, Grant had written Albert E. Church, Professor of Mathematics at West Point, for an appointment as an assistant professor.

Grant as a lieutenant in the 4th Infantry Regiment. The drawing was made from a photograph of Grant shortly after his arrival at the regiment, and was an illustration in Grant's memoirs. (AC)

Church was sufficiently impressed with Grant's abilities that he had agreed to take him when the current assistant's term expired. The opening occurred while Grant was in Mexico, and the appointment went elsewhere.

Grant's tenure in Louisiana ended in September 1845. Texas was annexed through a joint resolution of Congress in February 1845, with the bill signed by President James Polk on March 1, 1845. Orders to occupy the new state were sent during the summer, and the 4th Infantry accompanied the US force. For most of the war, Grant held a staff position as the 4th Infantry's quartermaster, a position he achieved thanks to the commander, Zachary Taylor. Worried about logistics, Taylor wanted energetic officers to fill the quartermaster posts, and had been impressed with Grant's energy at clearing underwater obstacles at Corpus Christi.

In many ways, his service as quartermaster served Grant's later career better than service in one of the regiment's line companies, even if – as Grant would have preferred – he had ended the war commanding a line company. The practical lessons he learned as quartermaster taught Grant the importance of logistics, and gave him an understanding of how to conduct logistical operations during fluid campaigning.

Quartermaster duties did not prevent Grant from seeing combat during the war. His regiment was present at the battles of Resaca de la Palma, Palo Alto, and Monterrey under Zachary Taylor, and he later participated in the invasion at Vera Cruz and the march to Mexico City under Winfield Scott.

At Resaca de la Palma, Grant led an infantry company in a successful charge against enemy positions. At Monterrey, Grant, who in his words, let "my curiosity get the better of my judgment," rode from his assigned position in the rear to see what was going on at the front. Once there, when the need arose for someone to carry a message over a hazardous route Grant volunteered. He succeeded in getting the message to its destination.

At Chapultepec, the final battle before the capture of Mexico City, Grant again took an active and this time a critical part in the battle. A Mexican field piece sited at a crossroad stalled the American attack. Grant collected a dozen volunteers to conduct a reconnaissance to find a way around the gun. During this he found an unengaged American field howitzer and a position from which it could flank the Mexican position – a belfry that would allow a howitzer to dominate the battlefield. Grant convinced the officer who controlled the gun to mount it in the belfry, and organized movement of the gun into the position. The gun, disassembled at the base, was carried up the stairwell and reassembled once up at the top of the tower. From there, it dropped shells on the Mexicans, forcing the Mexican artillery piece to withdraw.

At both Molino del Rey and Chapultepec Grant was brevetted for his initiative and bravery, ending the war as brevet captain (for Chapultepec) with the permanent rank of second lieutenant in the Regular Army. In many ways, the Mexican–American War – which Grant called an unholy and unjust war – represented the high point in his military career prior to the Civil War. The reluctant soldier had proved an excellent officer, and had gained favorable attention from his superiors.

Moreover, his experience in Mexico gave him first-hand knowledge of many of his principal adversaries, opponents, allies and rivals in the Civil War years. Over 200 West Point graduates – many of them his classmates, and others prominent during the Civil War – participated in the Mexican–American War, most of them in the army in which Grant served. He had watched future Confederate leaders, such as Robert E. Lee, Joe E. Johnston, Alfred Sidney Johnston, P. G. T. Beauregard, Gideon Pillow, Braxton Bragg, David E. Twiggs, and John Pemberton in action. Similarly, he observed the performance of future Union colleagues like George McClellan, George Meade, and Z. B. Tower. It gave him the measure of these men.

Additionally, the war gave Grant the opportunity to observe two excellent theater commanders – Zachary Taylor and Winfield Scott. He also learned how to conduct – and how not to conduct – field operations. At one point in the advance to the Texas–Mexico border, progress was stalled when the army reached a river without bridging equipment. Grant fumed at the delay, which he observed could have been avoided by a little foresight.

The Mexican War ended in 1848, and the 4th Infantry was withdrawn to Pascagoula, Mississippi, during July of that year. Grant immediately requested leave, and went to St. Louis, where on August 22, 1848, he married Julia Dent. Grant, a man that disliked the army, could honorably have left the United States Army at that point. The Army was downsizing following the war, and any officer that chose to leave could. He had served for six years, much of it in combat, discharging the obligation he had incurred by attending West Point. Instead, he decided to remain.

Why? Probably because he felt he had no real choice. He was now a married man, with a family to provide for. His wife came from a well-to-do family, and he felt the need to maintain the social level to which she was accustomed. When he had visited his family during his leave, he hinted that he would be open to working for some part of the family business, but his hints had been ignored.

The Army wanted Grant. He had been a star during the Mexican War. While an officer's pay was relatively low, it came regularly, and there were other, non-monetary benefits that went with the commission, including housing and servants. Additionally, an officer was a gentleman. Remaining in the Army gave him a social status unavailable in the civilian world.

Grant was a loving family man. In the era of the distant father and reserved husband, Grant was a hands-on parent and a doting spouse, but service in the peacetime army required long absences from his family – with disastrous consequences for Grant's career.

Initially, peacetime service was acceptable. The 4th Infantry was assigned to the Great Lakes as the 1840s closed and the 1850s began. Grant spent several years at Detroit, Michigan, and Sackets Harbor, New York, with his

When Grant's brigade commander asked for a volunteer to carry a critical message during the intense street fighting of the battle of Monterrey, Grant volunteered. He successfully delivered the message, despite being shot at dozens of times. (LOC)

wife able to live with him in both posts. By 1852 Grant's family had expanded by a son, and Julia was once again pregnant. Then, the 4th Infantry was reassigned to California.

Reaching California then required a hazardous ocean voyage around Cape Horn or across the Isthmus of Panama. Alternatively, one could cross the Great Plains and Continental Divide by wagon. The 4th Infantry took the quickest route, via Panama, but the Isthmus was one of the unhealthiest spots in the Americas, and pregnant Julia could not accompany him. Grant was lucky to survive the trip himself. One-seventh of those in Grant's party died of cholera crossing Panama.

Once the 4th Infantry was in California, Grant was unable to send for Julia and his children. His responsibilities as quartermaster increased. Following the Gold Rush of 1849, California was an expensive place, but Grant's regimental budget remained fixed. He was constantly on the move – which led to a succession of colds, and bouts of ill health. What was more, he heard from Julia and his family only infrequently. He learned of his second son's birth six months after the child was born. Nor could Grant afford to move his family closer. There were numerous business opportunities in California – opportunities other officers and sergeants in the 4th Infantry were able to cash in on. But Grant's business sense was abysmal. He lost money on everything in which he invested. As his debts mounted, his opportunity to bring his family to California dwindled.

The combination of loneliness, financial worries, and ill health left Grant depressed. Previously abstemious, in California Grant turned to drink. It was as much for his health as for solace – alcohol was then regarded as a cure for colds. But Grant could not hold his liquor, and even small amounts of drink incapacitated him.

Grant gained a reputation for drunkenness, although that alone would not have been enough to kill his career. Hard-drinking officers were an Army tradition. William Whistler, the 4th Infantry's colonel when the Mexican–American War started, was as notorious for his benders as his battlefield courage. Grant, who was well liked by virtually all his brother officers, had incurred the enmity of his immediate superior, Major Robert Buchanan, at his final post, Fort Humbolt near what is now Eureka, California. Buchanan, a martinet, compounded Grant's misery, jumping on his failings. Finally, on April 11, 1854, Grant sent a letter of resignation to Washington. It was sent only a few weeks after he had received word that he had been promoted to captain, then one of only 50 in the Regular Army.

Why did Grant resign? Rumor holds that Buchanan threatened Grant with court-martial for being drunk during a pay parade unless he resigned. This could be true, although no contemporary documents support that story. It could equally be that Grant, ill, lonely and fed-up with an unreasonable superior, did what he had threatened to do over the previous year. Regardless, the legend of a drunken Grant, drummed out of the Army for insobriety and incompetence, hovered around him for the rest of his life – and afterwards.

The failure years

Once Grant tendered his resignation he told his former colleagues that he planned to become a well-to-do Missouri farmer. Instead he spent seven years of frustrating failure. Returning to Missouri and his wife, who was staying with her father near St. Louis, proved challenging. He traveled to San Francisco to collect debts owed him, only to find his borrowers unable to pay. An old army buddy secured him free passage to New York City and Grant finally arrived in St. Louis after a side trip to Sackets Harbor to collect more money owed him. Hearing of Grant's arrival, the debtor skipped town, and avoided payment.

During the battle for Chapultepec, Grant persuaded the crew of a brass howitzer to emplace the gun in a bell tower. From there, Grant directed fire that helped turn the battle in favor of the Americans. (LOC)

Once in Missouri, Grant set out to become a successful farmer, working 60 acres that his wife received from her father as a wedding gift. Grant erected a cabin in 1856, puckishly naming the estate "Hardscrabble." Initially successful, his attempt at farming slid into disaster. The Panic of 1857 knocked the bottom out of farm prices. Missouri was a slave state, which Grant detested, and finding free labor to work his farm was difficult. While he tolerated ownership of slaves by his wife and her family for the sake of family peace, Grant was unwilling to lash slave labor to his own productivity. Grant sold Hardscrabble in 1859, with typical results. The buyer defaulted on the money he owed to Grant in 1860.

Other efforts proved equally unsuccessful. He entered a real-estate business with a cousin of Julia's in St. Louis. But business was slow in the aftermath of the Panic of 1857, and Grant was as unwilling to evict tenants unable to pay rent as he had been to lash slaves. He left the business after a year, taking a job at the St. Louis customs house.

He lost the customs house position after a month, and early in 1860 lost an opportunity to become St. Louis County Engineer. His antislavery views contributed to both disappointments. Between 1855, when Grant returned to Missouri, and 1860, the issue of slavery had become increasingly divisive. Grant outraged Missouri sensibilities by paying slaves who worked for him and freeing a male slave given to him as a gift. By 1860, disliking slavery was viewed in Missouri as virtually treasonous, even if that dislike was accompanied by grudging toleration.

During the years that he was failing as a farmer, Grant built Hardscrabble. The house was well built, but plain. Julia described it as a mere cabin. (LOC)

By then financial problems were pressing. Grant's household had grown to ten. Two more children had been born since his return from California. He also had to support four slaves owned by his wife. He turned to his father for help.

Jesse Grant's business had prospered during the years his eldest son was in the Army and playing farmer in Missouri. Grant's father owned stores in several towns, including a store in Galena, Illinois. Jesse mistrusted Ulysses's business sense and had resented his son's departure from the Army. An ardent abolitionist, he also despised the slave-owning Dent family, so his assistance since 1855 had been limited. As 1859 ended he offered his son a job at the Galena store – as a clerk. In April 1860 the Grant family – sans Julia's slaves, who were hired out – moved to Galena. Ulysses Grant took up his new station in life – behind the counter of a general store.

HOUR OF DESTINY

Had it not been for the Civil War, Grant would likely have finished his life in obscurity, at most a minor footnote in some graduate student's thesis on the Mexican–American War. Yet Abraham Lincoln's election to president in 1860 prompted seven southern states to secede from the United States and declare their independence. The new Confederate States of America – as these seven states styled themselves – were economically unviable. They had almost no industry, except for centers in Atlanta, Georgia, and New Orleans, Mississippi. But after South Carolina fired on Fort Sumter in Charleston Harbor on April 12, 1861, Lincoln issued a call for 75,000 volunteers. That led to the secession of four additional states from the Upper South who joined the Confederacy. Both sides began to arm.

A return to arms

Grant had lived in Galena, Illinois, for less than a year. He was known to have supported Stephen Douglas, the Democratic presidential candidate, over Lincoln. Elihu Washburne, Galena's Congressman, knew that, but he also knew Grant strongly opposed secession. Grant was the only man in the town who had been to West Point, and had seen combat in the Mexican–American War. When Galena held a meeting to raise soldiers to answer Lincoln's call for volunteers, Washburne maneuvered things so that Grant presided at the meeting.

Enough Galena men volunteered to raise two companies, rather than the expected one. Grant gained Washburne's support for the rest of the war, and was elected captain of one of the companies, but he demurred. He wanted command of a regiment, not a company, which required a colonel's commission, and those were issued by the governor – not by election. Grant stayed in Galena only long enough to organize and drill the new companies, and then left for Springfield, Illinois's capital, to seek a regiment.

He got his colonel's eagles – eventually. Initially, Illinois governor Richard Yates sidestepped his request because he heard Grant had left the Army under a cloud. Instead, Yates employed Grant filling out mustering paperwork for the volunteer regiments. Then Yates gave him the task of drilling the mustering regiments, but no colonel's commission, although Grant did well at both tasks. Disappointed, Grant went to St. Louis to see if he could find a command under Nathaniel Lyons, who had taken charge of Union forces there. Lyons, too, had heard the rumors about Grant and did not offer him a job.

Discouraged, Grant returned to Springfield. He wrote to Army Headquarters in Washington, DC, offering his services commanding a volunteer regiment. He never received a reply – the letter was misfiled. Next, Grant visited his father in Covington, Kentucky. Once there he went to Cincinnati, to seek a commission in Ohio. George McClellan, in charge there, remembered Grant from a meeting in California when Grant had been dead drunk. McClellan refused him. Charles White, with whom Grant had served in Mexico, offered to plead his case with Ohio's governor, William Dennison, a childhood friend of Grant's, but there were no promises.

Then, suddenly, Grant gained the regiment he had sought since mid-April. On June 15 Yates telegraphed Grant offering him command of an Illinois regiment. Grant immediately accepted. Later that day, he received the offer of command of the 12th Volunteer Ohio from Dennison. Grant, who had already packed, turned it down.

When Grant arrived in Springfield he learned that his new regiment, which would become the 21st Illinois, was a problem child: ill-disciplined and out of control. Grant had mustered the regiment in earlier as a 30-day unit. When asked to reenlist as a three-year unit, its men refused to serve under their incompetent colonel. Its officers, impressed with the quietly competent mustering officer, insisted on Grant. They had asked he be made their colonel when they mustered in. Yates, despite misgivings, agreed. The regiment was a dead loss as it stood. A "deadbeat" officer could hardly make things worse.

Grant surprised everyone other than himself and the officers of the 21st Illinois by quickly bringing the regiment back to order and turning it into a formidable fighting force. An unimposing figure, he wore an old slouch hat and a worn civilian suit while awaiting the colonel's uniform he had ordered. Yet his quiet self-confidence, his obvious competence, and the standards he set drew his men into obedience.

Soon Grant and his regiment were sent to Missouri. They were sent to confront a Confederate band under Thomas Harris. Hearing he was outnumbered, Grant, fearless on the plains of Mexico, found himself nervous

Grant's campaigns

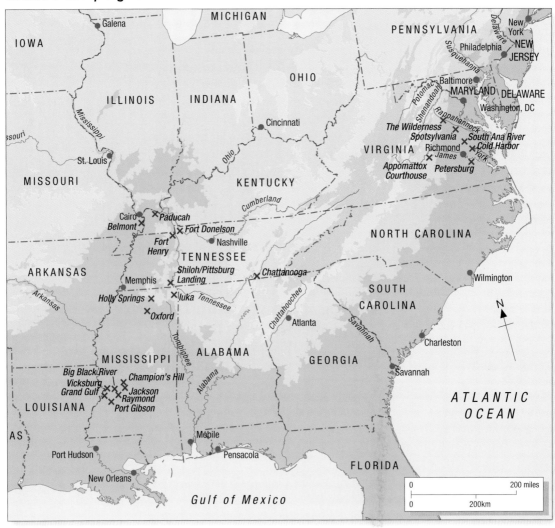

about the upcoming battle – not for his own safety as much as from fear that through his actions his men would come to harm. When he reached the enemy's encampment, he discovered the Confederates had skedaddled. Grant realized "that Harris had been as much afraid of me as I had been of him." After that Grant "never experienced trepidation upon confronting an enemy… I never forgot that he had as much reason to fear my forces."

Grant kept his regiment under strict discipline during the mission, preventing them from harassing or robbing Missouri civilians. He not only won the confidence of local civilians, but the higher command rewarded him, putting him in charge of several unruly volunteer regiments at Mexico, Missouri, effectively making him a brigade commander. Soon these regiments were as well disciplined as Grant's own.

In August, Grant learned he had been promoted to brigadier-general. Washburne added Grant's name to a list of Illinois volunteer brigadiers, placing Grant, first – and most senior – on the list. The promotion signaled that Grant had won over John Pope, who commanded the Illinois forces and one of those that had earlier warned Yates against employing Grant. Grant's brigade was sent to Ironton, Missouri, to protect the railroad junction from a rebel force, which was rumored to be twice the size of his force. After establishing control there, Grant was moved to Cape Girardeau in southeast Missouri. Then he was superseded in command by Brigadier-General Benjamin Prentiss.

Prentiss, junior to Grant, had been sent by John C. Frémont, then commanding in Missouri. Grant protested, but Frémont upheld Prentiss, and sent Grant to Jefferson City to chase down Confederate guerrillas. Then the War Department in Washington told Frémont that Grant was indeed senior to Prentiss. Embarrassed by the gaffe, Frémont recalled Grant, restoring him to his old command.

From Belmont to Forts Henry and Donelson

Frémont ordered Grant to Cairo, Illinois, and gave him responsibility for the region at the juncture of Missouri, Illinois, and Kentucky. When Grant took charge there, in late August 1861, Kentucky had declared neutrality. Lincoln, believing the first party to move into Kentucky would push it into the other camp, had ordered that neutrality respected.

In August 1861 Grant learned that he had been promoted to brigadier-general effective May 18, 1861 – largely through the influence of Illinois Representative Elihu Washburne. He is shown here, atypically, in a dress uniform. (AC)

On September 5, a Confederate force under Brigadier-General Gideon Pillow occupied Columbus, Kentucky, violating Kentucky's neutrality. Frémont ordered Grant to enter Kentucky and fortify the area south of Cairo. On receiving a report that Confederate forces were marching on Paducah, Kentucky, Grant interpreted these orders more broadly. Without waiting for instructions, Grant loaded up 1,500 troops in steamboats and occupied Paducah on the Ohio River, thus securing a major Northern supply line.

Grant remained at Cairo, straining to move against Confederate forces in Kentucky and central Missouri. With 13,000 men, he felt he had enough for offensive operations. Frustrated, he watched as the Confederates turned the strategically important Columbus into the "Gibraltar of the West." Finally, in late October, Grant received orders from Frémont to conduct a demonstration towards Belmont, Missouri, opposite the Mississippi River from Columbus.

Frémont intended for Grant to simply draw Confederate attention, without getting heavily involved. Grant planned to turn the demonstration into a battle. Lincoln relieved Frémont on November 2, leaving this command temporarily leaderless, and Grant seized his chance. On November 6 Grant heard reports that Confederate forces were occupying Belmont. He packed two brigades at Cairo into steamers for Belmont, unloading them three miles north of the town.

At the battle of Belmont, Grant's forces initially routed 2,500 Confederate troops under Gideon Pillow from their Belmont encampment. Grant's troops then succumbed to the temptation of souvenir hunting in the enemy camp. While the Yankees were celebrating victory, Leonidas Polk in

Columbus was preparing a counterattack. By the time Grant regained control, the Confederate attack was beginning. Grant kept his panicky men from routing, fighting a successful withdrawal to the boats, and returning to Cairo once the troops were reembarked.

Grant claimed Belmont as a victory, although losses were roughly even, and the Yankees had been chased out. Officially a demonstration, the post-battle withdrawal mattered less than if he had attacked Belmont with the stated intention of taking it. Yet Belmont was less of a victory than Grant claimed. He was lucky to have kept his force intact. He had lost control of his troops for a critical 30 minutes, placed his reserve too far away to help, and mishandled his cavalry.

Confederate forces were significantly larger than the Union troops, and Confederate casualties were marginally higher. Confederate forces were chased out of their encampment, while Grant managed a fighting withdrawal. Nevertheless, both the Army command and Northern newspapers willingly declared a victory without looking too closely.

Grant's mistakes mattered less than the lessons he learned from them. By demonstrating how vulnerable the position was to Union raiding, Belmont also discouraged Polk from sending forces deeper into Missouri.

Meanwhile, Grant had a new superior. Major-General Henry Halleck, who replaced Frémont, had also heard rumors about Grant and was inclined to believe the worst of what he heard, especially after meeting him. Grant's appearance was unimpressive. He was small, at only 5ft 8in. and 135 pounds. Perhaps taking after Zachary Taylor, Grant eschewed fancy uniforms. At first, like Taylor, he dressed in civilian clothing. After being ordered to wear a uniform, he took to wearing a private's tunic with officer's tabs attached and a plain and a worn Hardee hat. Moreover, Grant was softly spoken and diffident with senior officers.

Halleck set great store on the marks of rank, the gold braid and a military appearance, and to him, Grant neither looked like a general nor acted like one. Halleck, an intellectual, viewed the unscholarly Grant as a bumpkin. Moreover, Grant was aggressive. He could not be trusted not to chase off after the enemy, rather than adhering to a carefully thought-out battle plan – developed by Halleck. Halleck wanted Grant replaced with someone more suitable, but in view of Grant's political connections with Washburne and because Halleck felt there were more pressing issues in Missouri, he decided to wait for a better time. For three months – while Lincoln was urging Halleck to move into Kentucky – Halleck organized his department.

The battle of Belmont was inconclusive. Both sides claimed victory and rewarded the commanders involved. Its greatest value to the Union was the lessons it taught Grant – which he applied at Donelson and Shiloh. (LOC)

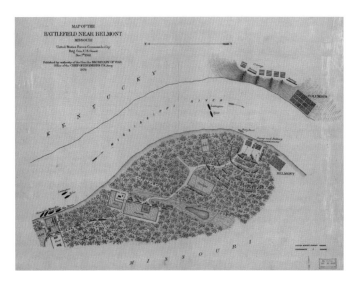

Three Confederate outposts were the keys to regaining Kentucky. Columbus, Kentucky, covered the Mississippi River, blocking further progress south. In 1861 the Confederacy built two forts in northern Tennessee to protect the state. Fort Henry guarded the Tennessee River on the Tennessee side of the point where the river formed the border between Kentucky and Tennessee. Fort Donelson, just northwest of Dover, Tennessee, blocked the Cumberland River, shielding Nashville, Tennessee's capital.

Grant learned that Fort Henry, on the Tennessee, was virtually defenseless, and visited Halleck on January 24, 1862, to urge an immediate attack. The commander of naval forces at Cairo, Flag Officer Andrew Foote, concurred with Grant's judgment, sending a telegram to Halleck, stating that with Grant's troops and the Foote's four armored gunboats they could take Fort Henry.

Grant recognized the mobility that the river system offered the army and made frequent use of eight steamboats to move his forces, especially during 1861 through 1863. (AC)

Halleck intended to attack Fort Henry, but felt that attacking before a set of mortar boats, capable of bombarding the fort with high-angle shellfire, had arrived would be premature. Further, Halleck intended to lead the attack, personally. Shortly after the meeting, he sent a message to Washington, requesting Grant's replacement.

Halleck suddenly reversed course after learning that 15 Confederate regiments, commanded by General P. G. T. Beauregard, were being transferred from Virginia to Tennessee. On January 30, Halleck ordered Grant to move immediately on Fort Henry and capture it.

Grant and Foote left Cairo on February 3, carrying Brigadier-General John McClernand's division. Unloaded at Itra Landing, in Tennessee, 8 miles downstream of Fort Henry before dawn on February 4, Grant and Foote took the transports back to Paducah, where Charles F. Smith's division was stationed. By February 5, it was at Itra Landing, too.

The next day Grant launched what he intended as a joint attack on Fort Henry, with his troops storming the fort as Foote's gunboats bombarded it. Heavy rains had soaked the area and troops became bogged down in deep mud as they attempted to reach Fort Henry. The gunboats attacked unsupported by the infantry and forced the Fort's surrender through bombardment alone. The heavy rains also flooded Henry's magazines and gun positions. McClernand's division, tasked with blocking Confederate retreat routes, failed to cut the roads, allowing 2,500 men in the garrison to escape to Fort Donelson. Only 92 Confederates, mostly wounded, were captured in the fort.

While the battle showed that Grant still had much to learn about combined operations, the result was a decisive victory. Taking Fort Henry opened the Tennessee River to the Union forces, but Grant was not satisfied with just Henry. He wanted Fort Donelson, too. The two forts were only 12 miles apart, but Foote's gunboats needed repairs, so Grant waited. On February 12, he marched on Donelson.

The Forts Henry and Donelson campaign

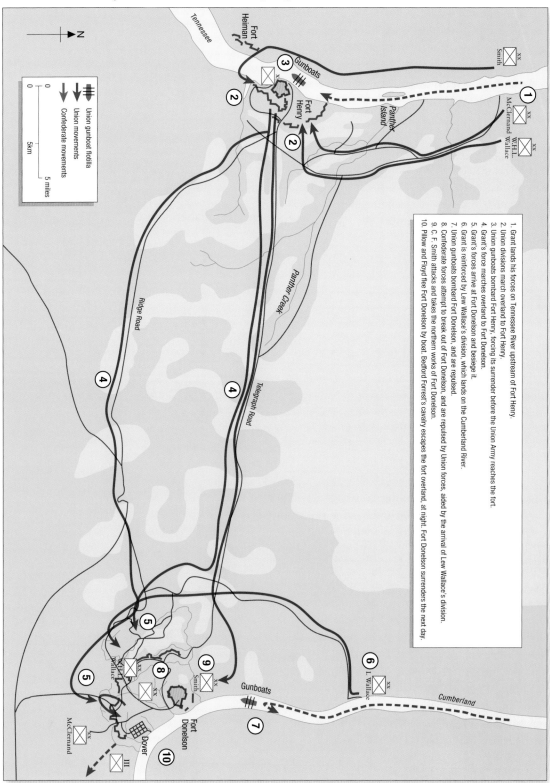

1. Grant lands his forces on Tennessee River upstream of Fort Henry.
2. Union divisions march overland to Fort Henry.
3. Union gunboats bombard Fort Henry, forcing its surrender before the Union Army reaches the fort.
4. Grant's force marches overland to Fort Donelson.
5. Grant's forces arrive at Fort Donelson and besiege it.
6. Grant is reinforced by Lew Wallace's division, which lands on the Cumberland River.
7. Union gunboats bombard Fort Donelson, and are repulsed.
8. Confederate forces attempt to break out of Fort Donelson, and are repulsed by Union forces, aided by the arrival of Lew Wallace's division.
9. C. F. Smith attacks and takes the northern works of Fort Donelson.
10. Pillow and Floyd flee Fort Donelson by boat. Bedford Forrest's cavalry escapes the fort overland, at night. Fort Donelson surrenders the next day.

Grant arrived on February 13, largely unmolested by Confederate forces in Donelson. Conditions were icy and cold, and Gideon Pillow, commanding at Donelson, had received sizable reinforcements. Technically John B. Floyd, who arrived with the reinforcements, had overall command, but he deferred to Pillow's greater military experience. If Donelson could be held, and Grant repulsed, Fort Henry's loss would be redeemed. The Confederates had roughly 16,000 men to Grant's 24,000. Grant had been reinforced by an additional division, commanded by Lew Wallace.

Grant attacked on the next day, using a plan similar to that which had taken Henry – bombard the fort with Foote's gunboats, and then walk in afterwards. This time, the fort's guns drove off Foote's flotilla. The next day, Grant considered the options. He did not want a siege and Foote wanted to withdraw his ships for repair, but he agreed to leave two gunboats to support the assault Grant planned. Before Grant could launch his assault, however, the Confederates attacked.

Pillow had panicked, and decided the fort was untenable. He convinced Floyd that the fort could not be held. At dawn, the Confederates launched an assault against McClernand's division, which was guarding the southern part of the Union arc around Donelson, poised to stop a breakout. . While the assault was initially successful, Grant counterattacked with Wallace's green division, blunting the Confederate drive and pushing it back into its fortifications.

Grant heard that the Confederate soldiers were carrying provisions during the attack. Realizing this meant the Confederates were attempting a breakout, he concluded that most of the Confederate army must be engaged on his right. He ordered Smith, commanding the division on the left flank, to attack the fortifications, stating that they could be taken by a prompt attack. Grant's judgment proved correct. Smith stormed and took those outer lines, leaving the Confederates with an untenable position. That night

Henry Halleck. Pop-eyed and over-cautious, Halleck wrote the Army's first book on strategy and tactics. He initially viewed Grant as over-aggressive and attempted to remove him. Unsatisfactory in the role of Commander of the Army, he proved a competent chief of staff for Grant when Grant became Commander of the Army. (LOC)

When Grant realized the Confederates were attempting to break out of Fort Donelson, he ordered Charles Smith, his one-time West Point instructor, to attack. Smith's assault took the outer works, making Donelson untenable. (LOC)

Pillow and Floyd fled in boats. Except for a small cavalry contingent that escaped, the rest of the garrison, commanded by Simon Bolivar Buckner, a prewar friend of Grant, asked for terms that night.

When Grant received the request, he replied, "No terms except an unconditional and immediate surrender can be accepted. I propose to move immediately upon your works." Buckner surrendered.

From Shiloh to Corinth

The capture of Forts Henry and Donelson were the first completely unambiguous major Union victories of the war, and they made Grant famous. A picture taken of him on Foote's flagship, holding a cigar given him by Foote became almost iconic. For the rest of the war, admirers sent Grant cigars. An occasional cigar smoker before Donelson, Grant became a heavy smoker afterward. Grant's cigars became as much a part of him as his beard and private's tunic.

The battles also earned Grant a new nickname – "Unconditional Surrender" Grant. His demand for an "unconditional and immediate surrender" struck a chord. Donelson also earned Grant Lincoln's favor. Lincoln found a general who was willing to fight – and win. Thereafter, Grant was under Lincoln's protection.

It did not gain what Grant wanted most, however: the immediate exploitation of the opportunities offered by the opening of the Tennessee River and Cumberland. Grant had 27,000 men, divided into four divisions commanded by Smith, McClernand, Wallace, and a new general, Stephen Hurlbut. Grant wanted to strike at both Nashville, the capital of Tennessee, and the Mississippi railroad junction at Corinth, Mississippi. Nashville, on the Cumberland, was undefended. Corinth was a short march from Pittsburg Landing on the Tennessee, and was equally open in February 1862.

Nashville fell within the territory of the Department of the Ohio commanded by the dilatory Don Carlos Buell. When Buell arrived, Grant visited him at Nashville to urge movement further south and east. Unfortunately, where Grant saw opportunity, Buell saw danger. Buell was more concerned with securing Nashville than pressing the enemy.

Worse, Halleck put Grant on a choke chain. Halleck was more convinced than ever that Grant was recklessly aggressive and wanted him gone. Halleck was incensed that Grant had gone to Nashville and was annoyed that he was not receiving regular dispatches from him. (Grant's dispatches were being intercepted by a Confederate sympathizer in the telegraph office and were destroyed before they reached Halleck.) With McClellan, the general-in-chief of the Union Army and another officer who disliked Grant, Halleck hatched a plot to remove him.

It was impossible to simply relieve Grant – he was too popular, and was the North's only unambiguously successful general. Instead, Halleck intended to remove Grant for cause. He began framing a case against Grant as insubordinate. Halleck circulated rumors that he was drinking again, although at this point Grant was still abstaining from alcohol.

The effort backfired spectacularly. Grant demanded a court of inquiry. This prompted Lincoln to request a list of specific charges against Grant. Halleck's accusations were all moonshine and McClellan, his ally in Washington, had just been relieved of his command after a disastrous performance in the Seven Days' Battle. Halleck retreated and insisted that Grant had misunderstood Halleck. Halleck telegrammed Grant, directing him to forget about the courts of inquiry, to take his army south, and win some more victories. Grant, a good soldier – and being ordered to do what he had wanted to do for over a month – quickly obeyed.

By the first week of April 1862, Grant had his army in southern Tennessee. Five divisions – those commanded by McClernand, Hurlbut, and three additional generals, William T. Sherman, Benjamin Prentiss, and W. H. L. Wallace, were at Pittsburg Landing. Lew Wallace's division was at Cump's Landing, 5 miles north. An additional division, William Nelson's, which belonged to Buell's army, was at Savannah, Tennessee, 2 miles downriver from Crump's Landing.

William T. Sherman. When Sherman joined Grant's command, shortly after Donelson's fall, he was under a cloud, and doubted his own ability. Under Grant's leadership he developed into one of the war's outstanding army commanders.

W. H. L. Wallace had taken over Smith's division. Smith, Grant's tactics instructor at West Point, and upon whom Grant had learned to rely, was dying from a leg infected after an accident. William Sherman replaced him as Grant's chief lieutenant. Sherman, a Halleck favorite, had won Grant's trust through a combination of competence and loyalty to Grant. Like Grant, Sherman's reputation was clouded. Sherman had been relieved of command earlier due to bizarre behavior, but under Grant he steadied. Grant put Sherman in charge at Pittsburg Landing.

Grant was at Pittsburg Landing waiting for the Army of the Ohio, commanded by Don Carlos Buell. One result of McClellan's fall was that Halleck had been given overall command in the west. Grant was given the Army of the Tennessee, with Buell subordinate to Halleck commanding the Army of the Ohio. Viewing Buell as a greater potential rival than Grant, Halleck gave Grant overall command of the move against Corinth. But while Grant sped to Pittsburg Landing, Buell crawled. Buell left Nashville on March 19. By April 6, only Nelson's Division had gotten as far south as Savannah.

The Union encampment at Pittsburg Landing was not entrenched. Grant considered ordering his troops to fortify it, but was dissuaded by the combined advice of Smith, Sherman, and Grant's engineering officer, James B. McPherson. Further, although Confederate cavalry had been active around the Union encampment since April 1, Sherman resolutely refused to believe that the Confederates were present in force.

A Confederate army – 40,000 strong – commanded by Albert Sidney Johnston had been in Corinth. Johnston was then considered the most capable general in the Confederacy, and proceeded to demonstrate why. Johnston had learned that Buell was joining Grant and realized that once merged, the Union forces would outnumber his own. Johnston resolved to strike before Buell's arrival, hoping to destroy Grant's army with a surprise attack. On Sunday, April 6, the thunderbolt struck. The attack caught the Army of the Tennessee unprepared.

The battle of Shiloh

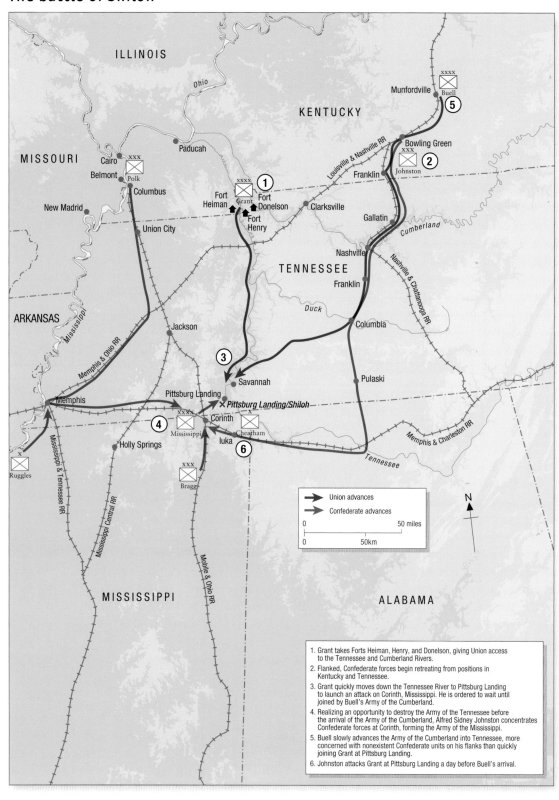

1. Grant takes Forts Heiman, Henry, and Donelson, giving Union access to the Tennessee and Cumberland Rivers.
2. Flanked, Confederate forces begin retreating from positions in Kentucky and Tennessee.
3. Grant quickly moves down the Tennessee River to Pittsburg Landing to launch an attack on Corinth, Mississippi. He is ordered to wait until joined by Buell's Army of the Cumberland.
4. Realizing an opportunity to destroy the Army of the Tennessee before the arrival of the Army of the Cumberland, Alfred Sidney Johnston concentrates Confederate forces at Corinth, forming the Army of the Mississippi.
5. Buell slowly advances the Army of the Cumberland into Tennessee, more concerned with nonexistent Confederate units on his flanks than quickly joining Grant at Pittsburg Landing.
6. Johnston attacks Grant at Pittsburg Landing a day before Buell's arrival.

The blow fell on the Union left, as Johnston wanted to drive the Yankees away from the Tennessee River and its naval support. At first the Confederate forces drove the Union back, destroying the unready regiments immediately before them. Grant, at Savannah, heard the noise of battle, and rushed to Pittsburg Landing by steamboat. Upon arrival, he found the Union army hard-pressed. Sherman had been working tirelessly to organize the Union defense, but Union forces were still being pushed back. Grant set to shoring up the Union center, reorganizing fugitives huddling at the river's edge, organizing an ammunition train, and collecting his artillery into a grand battery in the center of his line.

Moreover, Grant saw an opportunity on the first day to crush Johnston's army in a double envelopment. He ordered Lew Wallace at Crump's Landing to march on the Confederate left, and asked Nelson to move from Savannah to strike the Confederate right. Had either general moved promptly, Johnston's April 6 attack would have ended in defeat. Had both done so, Johnston's Army of the Mississippi would likely have been destroyed. Instead, Wallace got lost, while Nelson moved his division slowly, bickering with Grant.

The result was that Johnston almost succeeded in "watering our horses in the Tennessee." The Confederate attack stalled while attacking a defensive Union position in a sunken road. The Confederates continued attacking what they dubbed the Hornet's Nest, finally capturing a position they could have bypassed. Then Confederate troops wasted time looting the Union encampments. Grant's grand battery had time to assemble, and it stopped the Confederates.

Buell, arriving in advance of his army, saw numerous Union stragglers. He asked Grant if Grant was planning to withdraw. Grant, having sensed that the Confederate tide had crested, told Buell that he believed they would still win. By then Johnston was dead. Shot, he had bled to death, unaware of the severity of his wound until too late. Beauregard took command, and decided to halt the attack for the night. Victory could be achieved tomorrow.

All night long, Union reinforcements arrived; both Wallace's lost division and Buell's Army of the Ohio. Sherman approached Grant that night. "Well, Grant," Sherman said, "we've had the devil's own day of it, haven't we?" "Yes." Grant replied. "Lick 'em tomorrow, though." They did. The reinforced Union troops drove the exhausted Confederates from the field the next morning. Beauregard was forced to retreat back to Corinth.

Shiloh – named for a small church on the battlefield – was the bloodiest battle of the war to date. The Union suffered over 13,000 casualties; the Confederacy nearly 11,000. Although Grant's efforts had kept the army on the field throughout Sunday, he received most of the blame for being surprised, while Sherman and Buell received most of any credit for the victory. The Northern press accused Grant of having been drunk before and during the battle. Thereafter, Grant as a drunk became established as part of his image. In truth, it had been Grant's determination to fight on that salvaged a battle from which Buell and Sherman both favored retreat.

Worse humiliation followed. Halleck took over command of the combined armies, reducing Grant to a supernumerary role as an ignored second-in-command. Halleck then crawled to Corinth, taking four weeks to march 20 miles. When Halleck finally took Corinth, after it was evacuated, he discovered that the formidable artillery guarding the city was mostly painted tree trunks.

The campaigns for Vicksburg

One positive result of Halleck's capture of Corinth was that he felt comfortable restoring Grant to command. Halleck was moving to Washington, to become General-in-Chief of the Army. On July 17, Grant took charge of the Department of the Tennessee. At first he had to stand on the defensive, as much of his army had been drained away to reinforce Buell, back in central Tennessee and threatened by a new Confederate offensive.

Grant had an active view of defense, which consisted of striking at Confederate forces as they were concentrating. Thus, when Confederate General Stirling Price's army massed at Iuka, Mississippi, in September 1862, Grant attacked it. An attempted envelopment failed, but Price was driven out, and Grant followed up by taking Holly Springs, Mississippi, in November, again without achieving his goal of capturing the Confederate forces there. Grant took territory to facilitate destruction of Confederate field forces – not as an objective in and of itself.

Holding the two cities, especially Holly Springs, opened up central Mississippi to the North. One piece of territory Grant wanted was Vicksburg, Mississippi. A fortified town on the Mississippi, Vicksburg, along with Port Hudson, Louisiana, denied the North control of that river, allowing goods and troops to move to and from the eastern and western halves of the Confederacy. Taking Vicksburg would cut the Confederacy in half. It would also shorten Northern supply lines, making them less dependent on the rickety Southern railroad network. Finally, it was an objective that the Confederacy would fight to hold, giving Grant the opportunity to trap and destroy another Confederate army. Yet Holly Springs's capture led to another shakeup in Confederate command in Mississippi, with John Pemberton being given command of Confederate forces there.

Grant was also receiving reinforcements – of a kind. McClernand, long a thorn in Grant's side, had received permission in September from Lincoln to raise more troops in Illinois. McClernand thought this assignment would lead to him independently commanding the troops raised, a misconception Lincoln let ride in order to encourage McClernand's efforts. The ambiguity inspired McClernand's recruiting, however, and he raised enough regiments to fill two army corps.

Halleck took personal command of Grant's army after Shiloh, reducing Grant to a meaningless role as second-in-command. But Halleck's advance to Corinth, shown here, was conducted at a snail's pace – averaging less than a mile per day. (AC)

Lincoln also failed to completely clarify the situation with Grant, perhaps hoping to spur him on too. When Grant learned of McClernand's recruiting through press reports, Grant was already pushing down the Mississippi Central Railroad to Vicksburg. He got as far as Oxford, Mississippi, before the unreliable railroads prevented further advance. Seeking another route to Vicksburg, he gave Sherman an independent corps command, using Sherman's division and McClernand's newly raised formations to push down the Mississippi River, and attack Vicksburg from the north, at the mouth of the Yazoo River. Grant hoped the two-pronged attack would divide Confederate efforts.

As Grant waited in Oxford for supplies and railroad repairs, the Confederates struck. In December, Pemberton sent Earl Van Dorn with 3,500 cavalrymen to raid the Union rear. On December 20, having evaded Grant's cavalry, Van Dorn took Holly Springs and burned the Union supplies gathered there. The town should have been held, but the general commanding mismanaged preparations – despite a warning from Grant – and allowed his men to be surprised. Grant put his men in Oxford on short rations, and chose to fall back to Holly Springs until his supplies could be replaced. It was a decision he later regretted, as it meant that he had to fight for the same territory twice.

Meanwhile, Sherman was finding it hard-going in the swamps of the Yazoo bayous. Having arrived on December 26, he pushed through the swamps only to find himself checked at the heavily defended heights north of Vicksburg. After unsuccessfully attempting to flank the Walnut Hills, he finally launched a frontal assault on the Confederate positions on December 29. It was repulsed and Sherman withdrew back up the Mississippi.

McClernand and his corps had arrived at Memphis by the time Sherman returned there. McClernand, the senior general, appropriated Sherman's corps, and led both on an expedition to Arkansas Post, which fell on January 11, 1863. While Sherman had suggested the attack, it was launched without consulting Grant. It was also not the great victory McClernand claimed, as it pitted 33,000 Yankee soldiers and the Union river fleet against a bare 5,000 Confederates.

Grant was furious when he heard of the expedition, initially viewing it as a distraction. Later, he saw the advantage of removing a major enemy garrison in his rear. Yet McClernand was still a better politician than general. At the recommendation of both Sherman and Rear-Admiral David Porter, who commanded the naval forces on the Mississippi, Grant ordered McClernand to Milliken's Bend and Young's Point in Louisiana. Then Grant went there and took personal charge, over McClernand's objections.

While his new base at Milliken's Bend was physically closer to Vicksburg than Oxford, Grant was no closer to taking the city than he had been in October. He knew he could not take Vicksburg from the north or from the west across the Mississippi River. He needed to get south and east of the city. Since the Mississippi ran past Vicksburg he could not supply an army south of the city.

Grant decided to divert the river, cutting a canal across the neck of the oxbow that touched Vicksburg. The idea is not as unlikely as it sounds today. The Mississippi was constantly spontaneously changing course through such cuts, especially during the period of spring floods. Grant's reward for three months' effort was to have the river stubbornly ignore the new route when the cut was finished in late March. Several other attempts to flank the Vicksburg defenses by clearing new channels in the bayous north of Vicksburg also failed.

Grant's patience, never strong, ran out. He chose to move south of Vicksburg without securing a supply line. He decided to march his army down the Louisiana side of the Mississippi to Hard Times, Louisiana. From there it would be ferried across the river to Grand Gulf, Mississippi. McClernand's corps built a 70-mile timbered road from Milliken's Bend to Hard Times. While the army could not be fully supplied from it, enough ammunition could be moved to keep Grant's troops armed. Southern Mississippi was fertile farmland and Grant decided to obtain rations by foraging.

It was a bold plan, especially as it required the navy to run past Vicksburg's batteries. Until Vicksburg fell, these ships could not return to their bases. They would be cut off from repair and maintenance facilities. Yet Porter enthusiastically supported the plan, running the Vicksburg batteries at night and losing only one transport.

To ensure that his force could cross the Mississippi unmolested, Grant planned two diversions to distract Pemberton. A cavalry raid would cut across eastern Mississippi, drawing attention away from the great river, and a corps would feint an assault to take Haynes Bluff north of Vicksburg.

The campaign that followed exceeded expectations. The cavalry raid struck Newton Station in eastern Mississippi, on April 24. Conducted by Benjamin Grierson's cavalry Brigade, "Grierson's Raid" focused Confederate attention on the Mississippi railroads not the Mississippi River. Any remaining reserves Pemberton had were committed to forestall attempts by Sherman's Corps to take Haynes Bluff after a landing on April 29.

Second day at Shiloh

At the end of the first day of the battle of Shiloh, the Union Army had been pushed back almost to the Tennessee River. That night Sherman, found Grant, chewing on a cigar. "Well, Grant," said Sherman, "we've had the devil's own day, haven't we?" "Yes," Grant replied, "lick 'em tomorrow, though." The next morning, Grant delivered on that promise. On the Union left, Buell sent his army into the Confederate right. On the Union left Grant launched a dawn counterattack. Both assaults ultimately swept the Confederates from the field. Grant's assault started when Lew Wallace's division – absent the previous day – advanced across Tillman Creek. There, only 400 yards away, they surprised a Confederate brigade commanded by Colonel Preston Pond. Pond had failed to receive a fallback order issued by Beauregard the previous night. The startled and isolated Confederate brigade was greeted by a barrage from Union artillery batteries, and the sight of waves of Wallace's men crossing Tillman Creek.

On the same day, Grant was ferrying his army across the Mississippi at Grand Gulf. Rebuffed at Grand Gulf, he shifted to Bruinsburg, Mississippi, initially landing two corps, with 34,000 men. Then, in a series of five battles fought between April 29 and May 17 – Port Gibson, Raymond, Jackson, Champion Hill, and Big Black River Bridge – Grant's army marched north and east through Mississippi, muscling aside Confederate detachments sent to stop them. Following the Confederate defeat at Big Black River Bridge, Pemberton fell back into Vicksburg despite orders to evacuate the city.

Grant's plan to take Vicksburg from the south hinged on the Union's river fleet being south of Vicksburg. Once south of that city they would remain trapped south of Vicksburg until that town's capture. Regardless, the naval commander, David Porter, enthusiastically embraced Grant's plan, successfully bringing his ships past the Vicksburg batteries. (LOC)

A six-week siege resulted, after Grant tried twice, unsuccessfully, to storm Vicksburg. Rather than incur more casualties, Grant preferred to starve Pemberton out. The Confederacy tried to break the siege, and launched a raid on Milliken's Bend and Young's Point, hoping to repeat the results of Van Dorn's raid on Holly Springs. The attack was repulsed, but even if successful, Grant had moved his supply depot to Mississippi. Joseph Johnston, commanding the Department of the West, attempted to relieve Vicksburg, but he proceeded too cautiously. He got to the Big Black River on July 1, but was stopped by Sherman. It was too late. Vicksburg surrendered on July 4, 1863.

With the fall of Vicksburg, Union control of the Mississippi River was sealed. The one remaining fortified Confederate outpost on the river, Port Hudson, Louisiana, became untenable and surrendered on July 9. Grant captured 31,600 prisoners, 172 cannons, and 60,000 rifles. An additional 6,500 men were taken at Port Hudson. The South could not easily replace the lost ordnance, although the men captured were paroled.

The battle for central Tennessee

With the capture of Vicksburg, the pace of Grant's war slowed temporarily. The final element in his Vicksburg Campaign was to have been the destruction of Joseph Johnston's force sent to relieve Pemberton. But Grant's Army of the Tennessee had been exhausted by Vicksburg. While Sherman's corps was sent in pursuit of Johnston they stalled at Jackson, taking it with a short siege instead of the intended assault.

Elements of the Army of the Tennessee were being drawn off to reinforce other Union armies, reducing its size and striking power. When Halleck asked Grant to propose a new objective, Grant suggested Mobile, Alabama, striking down the route of the Gulf and Mobile Railroad. Mobile in summer 1863 was lightly held, and Grant's proposal would likely have worked. To Halleck, the concept was the wrong answer, and he directed Grant to drop it. So Grant spent the summer letting his army recuperate.

This pause ended in September. The Confederate losses at Vicksburg and Gettysburg in July had the paradoxical result of freeing up Confederate resources. The troops that fell back from Jackson, Mississippi, and Gettysburg, Pennsylvania, yielded a strategic reserve available for field operations. Loss of territories in the west meant these forces now covered a smaller area, permitting some to be committed to new offensive operations – with eastern and central Tennessee as the new focus point. Braxton Bragg had received reinforcements in central Tennessee. James Longstreet – a prewar friend of Grant's who had served in Grant's wedding party – had taken a portion of Robert E. Lee's Army of Northern Virginia to join Bragg. Troops were sent from Mississippi too.

At Jackson, Mississippi, Grant attacked and repulsed an army commanded by Joseph Johnston, which was attempting to relieve Vicksburg. This Union victory guaranteed Vicksburg's isolation and eventual fall. (LOC)

General William Rosencrans, a former subordinate of Grant, commanded the Union's Army of the Cumberland in central Tennessee. Rosencrans had become a hero in the Northern press following the battle of Iuka, where he commanded one division, but Grant was glad to see him go, believing that his actions – or rather inactions – had allowed the Confederate forces to escape at Iuka.

Rosencrans allowed himself to be surprised at Chickamagua Creek in north-central Georgia. On September 19 Bragg's Army of Tennessee struck the Union army. Rosencrans panicked, fleeing the battlefield, and stopping only when he reached Chattanooga, Tennessee, 12 miles away. Only the efforts of George Thomas, one of Rosencrans's corps commanders, prevented the Army of the Cumberland's destruction. As it was, Yankee forces were besieged in Chattanooga.

Grant was promoted to command of all Union forces west of the Appalachian Mountains, and told to clean up the mess in Tennessee. Grant gave Sherman command of the Army of the Tennessee, ordering him to central Tennessee. In addition, Secretary of War Staunton sent Joseph Hooker, former commander of the Army of the Potomac, to Tennessee with 15,000 men.

With reinforcements on the way, Grant then went to Louisville, Kentucky, to assess the situation. He found Chattanooga virtually cut off from supply and Rosencrans (in Lincoln's colorful description) "stunned like a duck hit on the head." Grant replaced Rosencrans with Thomas. On October 19, hearing rumors that withdrawal from Chattanooga was being considered, Grant sent Thomas a telegram stating: "Hold Chattanooga at all hazards. I will be there as soon as possible." Grant felt withdrawal from Chattanooga would be a mistake even greater than Grant's withdrawal from Oxford after Holly Springs. It would require unnecessary effort to regain ground already held.

Grant visited Chattanooga on October 23, making a two-day trip over the existing 60-mile supply route. He found the garrison of 45,000 outnumbered

The Vicksburg campaign

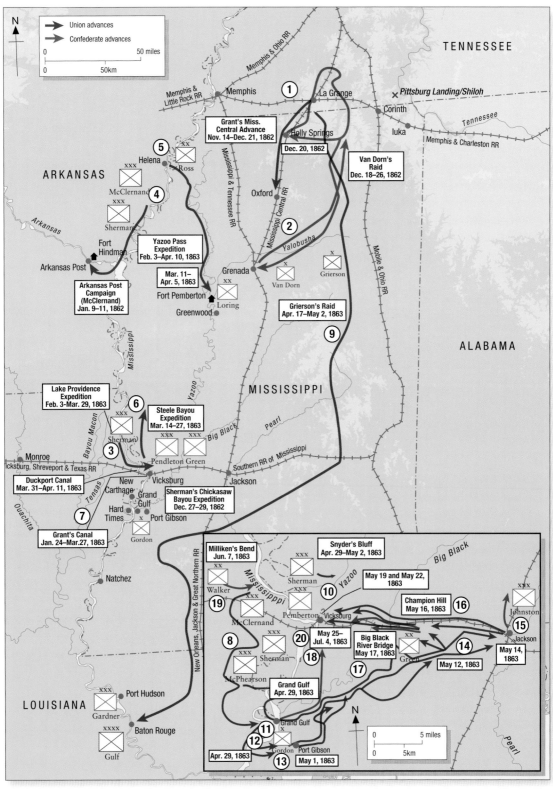

N

Union advances
Confederate advances

0   50 miles
0   50km

TENNESSEE

Memphis & Ohio RR

Memphis &
Little Rock RR

Memphis

1

La Grange

Pittsburg Landing/Shiloh

Corinth

Tennessee

Holly Springs

Grant's Miss.
Central Advance
Nov. 14–Dec. 21, 1862

Dec. 20, 1862

Iuka

Memphis & Charleston RR

Van Dorn's
Raid
Dec. 18–26, 1862

5

Helena

Ross

ARKANSAS

McClernand

xxx

Oxford

Mississippi & Tennessee RR

Mississippi Central RR

2

4

Sherman

xxx

Arkansas

Fort
Hindman

Arkansas Post

Yazoo Pass
Expedition
Feb. 3–Apr. 10, 1863

Mar. 11–
Apr. 5, 1863

Grenada

Yalobusha

Van Dorn

x

Grierson

x

Mobile & Ohio RR

Arkansas Post
Campaign
(McClernand)
Jan. 9–11, 1862

Fort Pemberton

Greenwood

Loring

xx

Grierson's Raid
Apr. 17–May 2, 1863

9

ALABAMA

Mississippi

Yazoo

MISSISSIPPI

Pearl

Lake Providence
Expedition
Feb. 3–Mar. 29, 1863

6

Steele Bayou
Expedition
Mar. 14–27, 1863

Bayou Macon

Sherman

xxx

Pendleton Green

xxx   xxx

Big Black

3

Monroe

Vicksburg, Shreveport & Texas RR

Southern RR of Mississippi

Duckport Canal
Mar. 31–Apr. 11, 1863

New
Carthage

Tensas

Vicksburg

Jackson

Grand
Gulf

7

Hard
Times

Port Gibson

Gordon

x

Sherman's Chickasaw
Bayou Expedition
Dec. 27–29, 1862

Grant's Canal
Jan. 24–Mar.27, 1863

Ouachita

Natchez

New Orleans, Jackson & Great Northern RR

Milliken's Bend
Jun. 7, 1863

Walker

xxx

19

Sherman

xxx

Snyder's Bluff
Apr. 29–May 2, 1863

xxx

Big Black

Yazoo

Mississippi

xxx

Pemberton

10

Vicksburg

May 19 and May 22,
1863

Champion Hill
May 16, 1863

16

Johnston

xxx

15

Jackson

McClernand

xxx

8

Sherman

xxx

20

May 25–
Jul. 4, 1863

18

Big Black
River Bridge
May 17, 1863

Green

xx

17

14

May 12, 1863

May 14,
1863

McPhearson

xxx

Grand Gulf
Apr. 29, 1863

N

0   5 miles
0   5km

Pearl

Port Hudson

Gardner

xxx

LOUISIANA

Baton Rouge

Gulf

xxxx

Grand Gulf

x

11

12

Gordon

Port Gibson

13

Apr. 29, 1863

May 1, 1863

by 70,000 Confederate troops entrenched in heights to the south and west of Chattanooga. Too few supplies could reach Chattanooga even to feed the troops, much less carry the ammunition and fuel they needed.

Grant's first steps helped develop a manageable supply line to Chattanooga. He had Hooker's troops take the Tennessee River crossing at Brown's Ferry on October 29, 1863. This reopened the Tennessee River to Kelly's Ferry. From there supplies could take a short road to Brown's Ferry, cross the Tennessee at a pontoon bridge, and travel by road to Chattanooga. This yielded a much shorter supply route, dubbed the "Cracker Line," to Chattanooga. At first, only food arrived in Chattanooga, followed by clothing and ammunition.

While Grant gathered his strength, Bragg diminished his. Ignoring the build-up of Northern forces, Bragg sent Longstreet's corps to eastern Tennessee with instructions to take Knoxville. Union forces there were commanded by Ambrose Burnside, another former commander of the Army of the Potomac. While Burnside was a less than stellar army or corps commander, he was competent in defense and did not panic. Instead, he wired Grant that Knoxville could be held, and suggested that Longstreet could be pulled further away from Chattanooga if Burnside retreated closer to Knoxville. Grant approved Burnside's initiative.

Grant twice attempted to take Vicksburg by storm. This painting shows the unsuccessful assault by the 13th Infantry on May 17, 1863. (USAHI)

1. Grant advances down the Mississippi Central Railroad line to Oxford Mississippi.
2. Van Dorn leads a cavalry raid that destroys Grant's supplies at Holly Springs, which forces Grant to retreat from Oxford back to Holly Springs.
3. Grant sends Sherman to capture Vicksburg via Chickasaw Bayou, to the north of Vicksburg. Sherman is repulsed.
4. Without notifying Grant, McClernand and Sherman move up the Arkansas River and capture Arkansas Post, AR.
5. Grant sends 11 infantry regiments, supported by Navy gunboats, down the Yazoo River in an attempt to reach Vicksburg via that route. The offensive is stopped at Fort Pemberton.
6. Grant attempts two more expeditions to establish a lodgment north of Vicksburg – Steele's Bayou Campaign, and the Lake Providence Campaign. Both are unsuccessful.
7. Grant moves his base of operations to Milliken's Bend, and then attempts to reroute the Mississippi River away from Vicksburg by digging a canal across one of the river's oxbow bends. The attempt fails when the canal fails to fill.
8. Grant assigns McClernand's XIII Corps to build a road from Milliken's Bend to Hard Times, LA. When the road is complete Grant marches the Army of the Tennessee down it to cross the Mississippi south of Vicksburg.
9. Grant sends Benjamin Grierson's cavalry brigade into eastern Mississippi as a strategic distraction. Grierson evades his pursuers, eventually arriving at Baton Rogue, LA.
10. Grant has Sherman's XV Corps launch a feint attack north of Vicksburg.
11. A Navy flotilla batters Confederate batteries at Grand Gulf into silence.
12. Grant crosses the Mississippi at Bruinsburg.
13. Battle of Port Gibson yields a Union victory, forcing Confederate forces to retreat, evacuating Grand Gulf.
14. Battle of Raymond. Grant forces Confederates under Pemberton's command to fall back to Champion's Hill.
15. Battle of Jackson forces Johnston's relieving army to retreat back to Alabama.
16. Battle of Champion Hill. Pemberton's forces retreat to Big Black River Bridge.
17. Battle of Big Black River Bridge. Union victory forces Pemberton back into fortifications around Vicksburg.
18. Grant arrives at Vicksburg, launches two unsuccessful assaults on the Confederate works and then besieges the city.
19. To raise the siege of Vicksburg, Walker's Texas Division attacks Milliken's Bend in an attempt to destroy Grant's supply depot. The attack is repulsed, but even if successful, it would have failed to destroy Grant's supplies, which had been moved into Mississippi in late May.
20. Out of supplies, Vicksburg surrenders to Grant on July 4, 1863.

George Thomas. A Virginian who stayed loyal to the United States, Thomas's resolute defense at Chickamauga prevented annihilation of the Union army and gained Thomas the sobriquet "the Rock of Chickamauga." While Grant viewed Thomas as too slow, at Chattanooga, he managed a feat Grant never achieved – destruction of a Confederate army on the battlefield. (LOC)

If Burnside was sanguine about retaining Knoxville, Washington was not. Grant was peppered with orders to relieve Burnside. This was impossible without using Sherman's army, which would not arrive before mid-November. Grant realized the best way to save Knoxville was not to send Burnside more troops, but rather to smash Bragg at Chattanooga. Grant focused on that.

Grant did not want to risk Lookout Valley, the key to protecting Chattanooga's supply line, by assaulting Lookout Mountain. A defeat might give the Confederates the chance to sweep the Union out of the valley in a counterattack. Grant's original plan was to take Missionary Ridge using the combined forces of Sherman and Thomas, while using Hooker's men to screen Lookout Mountain. Once Missionary Ridge was taken Lookout Mountain would be untenable.

The weather failed to cooperate with Grant's plan. As Sherman's troops arrived, heavy rains began falling, flooding the Tennessee River. The rains slowed movement, postponing the scheduled November 21 assault date. Additionally, on November 20, the pontoon bridge at Brown's Ferry broke. Sherman was forced to leave a division at Brown's Ferry. It was reassigned to Hooker's force.

Sherman snuck into Chattanooga undetected. While the Confederates observed the Army of the Tennessee at Brown's Ferry, part of Hooker's command had been concealed by hills blocking Confederate observation. Shortly after Sherman's men marched behind the hill, Howard's division, part of Hooker's command, marched out the other side to rejoin Hooker. The Confederates assumed that these were the same troops they observed earlier.

The assault was rescheduled for November 23, with modifications. Grant heard rumors that Bragg intended to withdraw and had Thomas attack Orchard Knob, the Confederate outpost in front of Missionary Ridge in the Confederate center. Thomas successfully took the objective, but confirmed that the Confederates were going to stand and fight. Because Orchard Knob offered a good view, Grant set up his headquarters there.

The battle of Big Black River Bridge

After landing at Port Gibson, Mississippi on May 1, 1863 – a move separating him from his supply lines – Grant fought an 18-day campaign across central Mississippi that drove from Port Gibson to Vicksburg. By May 17 Grant reached the Big Black River, where a Confederate army had entrenched in a horseshoe around the railroad bridge across the river. It was their last chance to prevent Vicksburg's investiture by Grant. The Confederate line was turned when Union Brigadier-General Michael K. Lawler took his 2nd Brigade into a meander scar that ran in front of the left flank of the Confederate line. Using this former riverbed to shelter them, Lawler led his brigade unseen 100 yards from the enemy lines. They then fixed bayonets, left the meander bed, and charged across a field to the Confederate works. The charge took the entrenchments and forced the Confederates across the river. Vicksburg was now isolated from the rest of the Confederacy.

Grant took personal charge at Chattanooga, first ensuring that a secure supply line existed, and later planning the successful Union assault on the besiegers. This picture shows Grant at Lookout Mountain shortly after the battle. (LOC)

The next day, Sherman attacked the Confederate right, anchored on the end of Missionary Ridge, while Hooker launched a "demonstration" at Lookout Mountain. Since Hooker had been strengthened by one division Grant gave permission to modify the demonstration to an assault – if it proved practical. Hooker took this as permission to assault Lookout Mountain, and did. While the Confederates were entrenched, they were outnumbered six to one. Fought in a foggy mist, Hooker swept the Confederates off the hill in a fight romantically called "the battle above the Clouds."

Meanwhile, Sherman struck Missionary Ridge, launching a successful surprise attack across the Tennessee River. Upon taking the position, he received a nasty surprise himself. He had not attacked Missionary Ridge. The Confederate right was on a different hill, separated from Missionary Ridge by a wide depression. It was a good jumping-off point for a future assault on the ridge, but his men would have to fight uphill.

On the 25th Grant launched his final assault on Missionary Ridge. Sherman struck the ridge from his position on the Battery Heights, which he had taken the previous day. The Confederates had hastily fortified their position against this threat the previous night, and fought doggedly to keep it, even rolling rocks on Sherman's men. After six hours of assault, Sherman called off the attack. Hooker's assault on the Confederate left was stalled by burned bridges, which slowed his advance.

Wanting to pull attention away from Sherman, Grant ordered Thomas to demonstrate against the Confederate center, although he did not want the center assaulted. Going up the steep heights with no cover would have been suicidal – a Yankee version of Pickett's Charge. Once Thomas's units reached the foot of the ridge, they began climbing, determined to reach the enemy. Furious, Grant gave orders for the men to fall back, orders Thomas passed forward, only to have them ignored. This time the men knew better than the generals. As the blue lines swarmed up the slope, Bragg's army panicked and ran. The siege of Chattanooga was lifted, and Grant was victorious.

Commander of the Army

In the wake of the Confederate rout, Grant sensed an opportunity to annihilate an army in the field. Grant used Hooker, largely unengaged on the last day at Chattanooga, in pursuit. Hooker pursued, but the Confederate rearguard, a division commanded by Patrick Cleburne which had stubbornly held Missionary Ridge against Sherman, fought equally hard against the advancing Yankees. Hooker was checked at Rossville Gap, and with his troops weary, worried about outrunning his supplies, and needing to relieve Knoxville, Grant halted his pursuit.

Burnside, perhaps the only one unworried about the North's ability to hold Knoxville, was still hanging on, his ability to resist limited only by his supply of food. When Grant started his assault on Bragg's positions around Chattanooga, Grant thought Burnside had about two weeks' worth of provisions. As soon as Missionary Ridge fell, Grant sent a corps from Thomas's army, commanded by Gordon Granger, to relieve Knoxville. Granger's advance was laggardly. Fearing that Granger would not arrive in time, Grant reassigned the pursuit to Sherman, who aggressively pushed to Knoxville.

Sherman's speed proved unnecessary. Upon hearing of Bragg's defeat, Longstreet lifted the siege and withdrew east. Close to the border of his native North Carolina, and far from Knoxville, Longstreet put his corps into winter quarters. Bragg was relieved of command and replaced by Joseph Johnston, a general whose skills Grant respected far more than Bragg's.

With the situation in Tennessee settled, Grant set about cleaning up the rest of the west. Sherman had not brought the whole Army of the Tennessee with him, so Grant sent him back to Mississippi to clear out Confederate holdouts there. To free up forces for a spring offensive into Georgia, Grant wound down the Red River campaign, halting it at Shreveport. He initially considered sending Thomas after Longstreet, but after further consideration decided that Longstreet's army was of less use to the Confederacy in far-eastern Tennessee than it would be elsewhere, and chose to leave it unmolested.

In February 1864, Congress restored the rank of lieutenant-general of the army, previously only held as a permanent rank by George Washington and dormant since then, except for a brevet commission granted to Winfield Scott in 1856. Grant, of course, was the first Army officer to receive the rank, effective March 9, 1864. Lincoln's motivation for supporting the legislation was less to reward Grant for his victories at Vicksburg and Chattanooga than to make him the ranking officer in the United States Army.

Lincoln had sought a commander willing to fight and capable of winning for three long years. In Grant he sensed he had found his man. As early as the spring of 1862 Lincoln wanted Grant in a combat command. When Halleck and McClellan had tried to maneuver Grant out of the Army, Lincoln's response was "I can't spare this man. He fights." Two years later Grant had demonstrated – repeatedly – that not only was he willing to fight, he won when he fought. Lincoln also realized that Grant's ability to win battles had repeatedly been hobbled by timid and less talented superiors. Making Grant the United States Army's first lieutenant-general meant that could never happen again. Lincoln had Grant where he wanted him – as General-in-Chief of the United States Army.

Lincoln wanted an opportunity to meet his new commander. The two men had conversed via telegraph on several occasions, yet despite both being from Illinois the two had never met. Grant was called to Washington to receive his new rank at a ceremony at the White House on March 9, 1864.

Arriving at Washington with his eldest son, Frank, Grant was dressed, as usual, in a private's uniform with general's tabs pinned to the shoulders.

The ordered demonstration of Thomas's corps at Missionary Ridge turned into an unordered – and successful – assault on Confederate forces entrenched atop the ridge. Grant was horrified when he saw the charge develop, expecting a slaughter on the scale of Marye's Heights at Fredericksburg or Pickett's Charge at Gettysburg. (LOC)

The desk clerk at the Washington treated this unimposing guest with disdain, offering him a spare room in the attic. It was not until the clerk saw the guest's name that he realized who he was snubbing. Grant was immediately given a first-class room.

Grant discovered that he had become famous – and that he detested fame. He could no longer eat a meal undisturbed in public, and was constantly being asked to speak, something the taciturn general hated. But Grant also discovered that he liked Lincoln. Unlike previous superiors, Lincoln told Grant only one thing – win the war. Grant had worried that Lincoln would micromanage his efforts, knowing that he had hectored previous generals-in-chief with a blizzard of suggestions as to how to conduct the war. But Lincoln had pestered McClellan and Halleck in order to prod them into action, and he realized that this was unnecessary with Grant. Lincoln's main reason for appointing Grant was so that he could stop playing general himself, a task for which the president felt inadequate, even given the poor quality of Grant's predecessors.

Given a free hand, Grant restructured both the Union's grand strategy and the Army. He created the first coherent national strategy for the Army. Rather than focusing on territory Grant wanted the Army to concentrate on the Confederacy's field forces. Destroy the Confederate armies and the Confederacy would have to surrender. At the start of 1864 the Confederacy had two field armies: the Army of Northern Virginia, commanded by Robert E. Lee, and the Army of Tennessee, led by Joe Johnston.

Grant also restructured the Union Army, although he left the Army of the Potomac largely intact, retaining George Meade, victor of Gettysburg, in overall command and keeping most of its corps commanders in their posts. One change he did make was to place Sherman's most talented divisional commander, Philip Sheridan, in charge of the Army of the Potomac's Cavalry Corps. Sheridan had always previously served in the infantry, but he had a natural aggressiveness necessary for a successful cavalry leader.

Other Grant protégés were similarly promoted. Sherman filled in for Grant as overall commander in the west, with James McPherson replacing Sherman in command of the Army of the Tennessee. Thomas continued in command of the Army of the Cumberland, subordinate to Sherman, while Ambrose Burnside's IX Corps was brought back from Tennessee to Northern Virginia, as an independent command. IX Corps was not merged with the Army of the Potomac because Burnside was senior to Meade.

Henry Halleck, Grant's long time superior, was shifted sideways, to be chief of staff for the Army. It was a role for which Halleck was better suited than commander-of-armies, and he did outstanding work in that office. Grant was forced to keep Benjamin Butler, a controversial political general, in command of the Army of the James. The Army of the James was to play an important role in Grant's plan, and he wanted an officer he could trust in charge of it. But Butler was a "War Democrat," and a competent military administrator, so Grant could not replace him. Butler would prove a wretched field commander.

Grant had some geographic objectives. He targeted the South's remaining industrial base – northern Georgia around Atlanta and the Confederate capital of Richmond, Virginia. Unlike his predecessors he was less interested in taking these cities than in destroying their manufacturing capacity. Once the factories were razed,

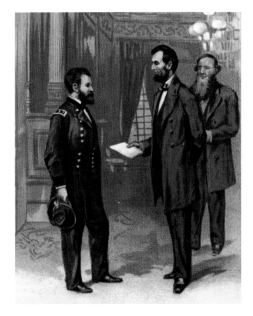

Grant first met Lincoln on March 9, 1864, when the President awarded his commission as a lieutenant-general. The two had become friends prior to that meeting, sharing a mutual admiration for the other's ability, and through a correspondence conducted via telegraph. (LOC)

holding these cities was unimportant. Similarly, he wanted the Shenandoah Valley of Virginia either under Union control or with its agricultural capacity destroyed. The Valley was the breadbasket and commissary for the Army of Northern Virginia. Without its food, Lee's army would starve. The South's remaining open ports – Mobile, Alabama, Charleston, South Carolina, and Wilmington, North Carolina – were also targets, for similar reasons. Taking them would deny the South its final overseas sources of supply.

As the campaign season of 1864 began, Grant had his plan in hand. Sherman would go after Johnston and Atlanta. Meade would concentrate on Lee and Richmond. Franz Sigel, another political general, commanding the Department of West Virginia, was given the task of clearing the Shenandoah. The rest of the Union armies required to garrison captured Confederate territories were also to advance. As Grant put it, "by advancing they would compel the enemy to keep detachments to hold them back, or else lay his own territory open to invasion." Lincoln pithily summed up Grant's approach: "if a man can't skin he must hold a leg while somebody else does."

From the Wilderness to Petersburg

From a strategic standpoint, the advance into Georgia and against Joe Johnston's army was the most decisive thrust. Grant chose to attach himself to Meade's Army of the Potomac rather than Sherman's western command that would be moving on Atlanta. There were several reasons that he made this choice. The biggest one was that he had more faith in Sherman and his western forces than he did in Meade and the Army of the Potomac.

Grant had watched the Army of the Tennessee and the Army of the Cumberland in action, and knew they could move swiftly and were used to winning. By 1864 Grant had boundless confidence in Sherman. On the other hand, the Army of the Potomac lost much more often than they won,

James B. McPherson had been Grant's engineering officer at Shiloh. He later developed into one of Grant's most effective corps commanders. Marked for higher command by Grant, McPherson died in battle during the Atlanta campaign. (AC)

and moved extremely slowly. After Gettysburg, with Lee's army pinned against a flooded river, Meade had held the Army of the Potomac back, permitting the Army of Virginia to survive. While Meade achieved the tactical objective of removing Confederate forces from Pennsylvania, he missed a larger strategic opportunity. To Grant that was indefensible. Since remaining in contact with the Confederate field armies was a key to Grant's overall strategy, he chose to attach himself to the army he felt was least likely to pursue the enemy aggressively.

There were other reasons too. Washington was the administrative center of the Army. Trying to manage the army from Tennessee, even with the capable Halleck as chief of staff in Washington, would be difficult. Finally, the very fact that the Virginia front was less important than Georgia gave Grant an opportunity for strategic deception. By 1864 the Confederacy believed Grant to be the Union's best general and felt that Grant just had to be in the spot most critical to the Union. That meant Grant's presence in the East distracted attention from the West. Grant was playing the game on a national scale, and if he could score points by giving the ball to someone else, that was fine. Victory was more important to Grant than who got the credit for it.

Grant's grand strategy was put into motion in May 1864. Four armies maneuvered against the Confederacy. In Tennessee Sherman began a march that would end in Atlanta by September. Sigel began his march down the Shenandoah. Grant prodded the Army of the Potomac south, while Butler pushed the Army of the James up the James Peninsula. The stated goal of these moves was the capture of Richmond. Its actual objective was the destruction of Lee's army, with Butler's army as the anvil and Meade's as the hammer.

Anvils proved hard to move. Butler got as far as Drewry's Bluff before his army was attacked by a smaller force commanded by Beauregard. Although Butler's army was 40 percent larger than Beauregard's, Butler immediately entrenched, choosing an easily defended neck between the James and Appomattox rivers. It served Beauregard equally well for that purpose and his army dug in too, trapping Butler's troops. By May 16, the Army of the James was trapped, in Grant's words "as if it has been in a bottle, strongly corked."

Meade's army, with Grant in attendance, began marching south on the same day as Butler's started west, May 4. Grant intended to flank Lee's army, located at Mine Run. To march around Lee's left would leave Washington open to attack, even with Burnside's independent corps to cover the capital. It was also the longer route, a worry given the Army of the Potomac's deliberate pace. The alternative was to move around Lee's right. To flank Lee's right Grant would have to pass through a narrow band between Lee's Army and the Rappahannock River. That band was filled with tangled thickets, known as the Wilderness. The year before, the Army of the Potomac had fought Lee's army in the same spot, resulting in a thumping defeat at Chancellorsville.

Grant chose the eastern route, gambling that he could march the army through the Wilderness before Lee could react, forcing a battle in the open terrain south of these dark woods. He underestimated both the ability of the Army of the Potomac to delay even a simple march and Lee's reaction time.

The result was a two-day meeting engagement fought on May 5 and 6. Known as the battle of the Wilderness, it was virtually a rerun of the battle of Chancellorsville. Union forces were hammered by Lee's counterattacks, and Confederate pickets shot another Southern corps commander.

James Longstreet was wounded within a mile of the spot where Thomas "Stonewall" Jackson had been fatally wounded a year earlier. Longstreet eventually recovered, but many of those wounded on the first day – on both sides – were trapped when the woods in which the previous day's fighting took place caught fire. Those unable to move burned to death.

Grant had been licked as badly before – on the first day at Shiloh, and on his several unsuccessful attempts to take Vicksburg. The army was still capable of fighting. As long as Grant could keep Lee's army in the field it could replace its losses. Even at the unfavorable exchange rate the Union Army suffered at the Wilderness, Lee would run out of men first. At the battle's end, Grant ordered the Army south, again hoping to flank Lee's right.

The move transformed a drubbing worse than the Army of the Potomac suffered at Chancellorsville into a Union victory. Morale among the soldiers of the army soared. For the first time Bobby Lee's army had not forced them back.

However, Lee again beat the slower moving Union army to their new destination, Spotsylvania Courthouse. Lee was already entrenched by the time Grant arrived on May 8. Grant assaulted the Confederate defenses several times over the next ten days. Union casualties were heavier than those of the Confederacy, but Union losses could be replaced while Confederate losses could not.

On May 9, Grant permitted Sheridan to take his corps on a cavalry raid towards Richmond. Sherman swept across Virginia, meeting and defeating the cavalry of the Army of Northern Virginia at Yellow Tavern, where J. E. B. Stuart, the Confederate cavalry commander was killed. Sheridan rode down to Butler's command, resupplied, and returned to Grant on May 24.

By then both Confederate and Union armies were at the North Anna River. Grant had again attempted to flank Lee, and Lee had again disengaged and beaten Grant south. Grant again faced Lee's army in a fortified position. While Grant tested Lee's line with an assault, this time he only waited two days before attempting to flank Lee yet one more time. Ominously for Lee, losses at South Anna were roughly even.

The two armies again raced for a confrontation. This time the destination was Cold Harbor, 5 miles east of Richmond. Part of Burnside's Army, XVIII Corps, commanded by William F. "Baldy" Smith, marched north to join Grant, who arrived on May 31, only to find he had been outmarched by Lee yet again. Initially, Grant's generals thought Lee could be beaten by a direct assault. By now Grant was skeptical, but agreed if the assault were made immediately before Lee was fully dug in.

It might have been a good gamble on June 1, when Lee was so badly outnumbered that he had no reserves. His entire army was committed to the front. But Grant's subordinate commanders postponed the assault until June 3. Not wishing to override them, Grant allowed the attack to proceed.

Philip Sheridan. Little Phil was only 5ft 5in. tall, but was a giant as a military commander. While Sheridan had only commanded infantry prior to 1864, Grant gave him command of the Army of the Potomac's Cavalry Corps, and later an independent command in the Shenandoah. (AC)

Grant's Overland Campaign

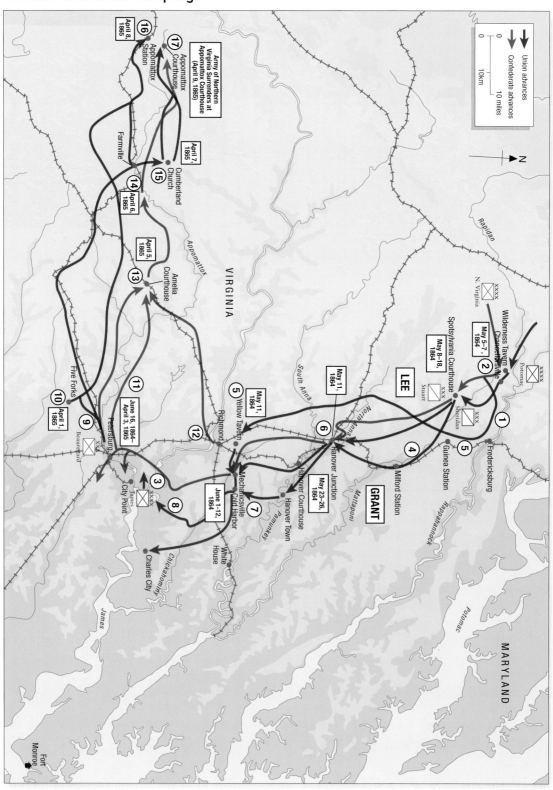

Army of Northern Virginia Surrenders at Appomattox Courthouse (April 9, 1865)

It was a disaster. Lee's engineers had two days to prepare and the Union attack was uncoordinated. Union soldiers were mowed down in thousands without making any progress against Lee.

Grant spent an additional ten days at Cold Harbor, but attempted no further frontal assaults on Lee's trenches. In his memoirs Grant stated "I have always regretted that the last assault at Cold Harbor was ever made. At Cold Harbor no advantage whatever was gained to compensate for the heavy loss we sustained." Grant would be reluctant to order frontal attacks on prepared entrenchments again. Maneuver was his preferred solution, so he again attempted to flank Lee's right. This time Grant did surprise Lee. Lee assumed that Grant would attempt to join forces with Butler's Army of the James.

Instead, Grant headed to Petersburg. Building the longest pontoon bridge of the war, his army crossed the James River unexpectedly. A race developed, with Grant in the lead for the first time. Again, the slow-moving commanders of the Union's eastern armies defeated Grant's intentions. The race to Petersburg started on June 9 when Butler, as ordered, moved his army against the Petersburg fortification. While formidable, they were almost empty. Only a brigade of regulars and a hastily assembled militia of boys and old men from Petersburg were in the trenches. Yet this was enough to bluff Butler, and deter him from making an assault that would have taken the works and made Petersburg untenable to the Confederates.

Grant's first battle with the Army of the Potomac was the bloody battle of the Wilderness, fought at virtually the same spot as the previous year's defeat at Chancellorsville. Its horror was compounded when the woods caught fire. Shown here is the evacuation of the wounded from the burning woods. (AC)

1. Grant moves the Army of the Potomac south across the Rappahannock and Rapidan Rivers, hoping to flank the Army of Northern Virginia before they can react. (May 3, 1864)
2. Lee catches Grant's Army at the Wilderness. A two-day battle ensues. (May 5–7)
3. Benjamin Butler lands the Army of the James at Bermuda's Hundred, and begins marching to Petersburg. He is soon stopped at the neck between James and Appomattox Rivers by a corps-sized force commanded by P. T. G. Beauregard.
4. Grant moves south after the battle of the Wilderness. Lee again outmarches the Army of the Potomac and entrenches at Spotsylvania Courthouse, where a ten-day battle is fought. (May 8–18, 1864)
5. Grant detaches Sheridan's cavalry corps on a raid to Richmond. Lee sends J. E. B. Stuart's cavalry in pursuit. A cavalry battle at Yellow Tavern leads to the death of Stuart. Sheridan takes his corps to join the Army of the James, then returns to Grant. (May 9–14)
6. Grant again tries to flank Lee, who catches Grant at Hanover Junction. The battle of South Anna is fought there from May 23 to 26, 1864.
7. Grant moves to Cold Harbor attempting to flank Lee. Grant's corps commanders launch a direct assault against Lee's entrenched army and suffer devastating losses. (June 1–12, 1864)
8. Grant again attempts to flank Lee, moving around the Army of the James to attack Petersburg. He outmarches Lee, but his corps commanders hesitate at attacking the lightly manned Petersburg works. By the time they are willing to attack, the Army of Northern Virginia arrives in Petersburg. (June 12–16, 1864)
9. Unwilling to storm Petersburg, Grant besieges the town. The siege lines grow to 53 miles by the end of the siege. (June 16, 1864–April 3, 1865)
10. Petersburg is flanked at the battle of Five Forks. (April 1, 1865)
11. Lee withdraws from Petersburg. (April 2–3, 1865)
12. Richmond falls. (April 3, 1864)
13. Grant pursues the Army of Northern Virginia. Union and Confederate cavalry clash at Amelia Springs. Lee is cut off from Danville. (April 5, 1865)
14. A quarter of Lee's army is captured at a battle at Sayler's Creek. (April 6, 1865)
15. The Confederate rearguard fight the Union vanguard at Cumberland Church. (April 7, 1865)
16. Sheridan's cavalry capture Confederate stores and rations at Appomattox Station before Lee can reach them, cutting Lee's Army off from supplies. (April 8, 1865)
17. Having lost much of his army, and lacking supplies, Lee surrenders the remaining Army of Northern Virginia to Grant at Appomattox Courthouse. (April 9, 1865)

Then, on June 15, the two lead corps of Grant's army arrived. They, too, outnumbered the Confederate forces then present at Petersburg. Smith's XVIII Corps made a halfhearted assault on that day, but Smith called it off when rumors of Confederate reinforcements reached him. Smith wanted no repetition of the slaughter at Cold Harbor, and talked Winfield Hancock, commanding the other corps, into delaying an attack.

The siege of Petersburg to victory at Appomattox

The pause was fatal. Had the two corps struck, they would have taken the entrenchments protecting Petersburg. By waiting, they gave Lee enough time to reach the works. By the time Grant's full force arrived at Petersburg on June 18, the moment had passed. Grant would not authorize an attack on the fully manned Confederate works. Nor could he again move left against Lee's right. He had run out of room.

Instead, Grant besieged Petersburg. While Grant kept engaged with Lee's army it could not recuperate, and would grow steadily weaker. As long as Grant threatened Richmond, Lee would keep his army at Petersburg. And Grant could keep up the pressure by slowly extending his lines to the left with the goal of cutting off the railroads that ran to Richmond. Eventually the siege lines would stretch 53 miles.

The siege lasted nine months. Petersburg was never invested, as the Union lines never reached more than two-thirds around the town, even at the end of the siege. Yet even this seemingly static situation contributed to Grant's overall plan, tying up the South's most experienced army and commander far from more critical fronts. Over the rest of the country much was happening.

The Shenandoah campaign had started well, but then gone badly. Sigel reached New Market on May 15, only to be decisively defeated and pushed north. Grant replaced Sigel with General David Hunter, who started a new push south in June. After this force captured Staunton, and headed for Lynchburg, Lee detached a corps from his army, commanded by Jubal Early. Early relieved Lynchburg, chased Hunter into West Virginia, and marched on Washington, DC. Early knew he lacked the strength to take Washington, but the Yankees did not. Pressured by Washington, Grant in turn was forced to detach a corps to defend Washington. The corps arrived too late to intercept Early, who was already marching back to the Shenandoah Valley after putting a scare into Washington.

During this period, the first serious attempt to storm the Petersburg siege lines occurred. A Pennsylvania regiment, made up mostly of coal miners, spent over a month digging a tunnel under the Confederate lines. The resulting mine was massive. When detonated, it created a crater 170ft long by 60ft wide that was 25ft deep. The July 30 assault on the crater was badly executed. Black troops trained to scale the crater were replaced with white soldiers because Grant feared the political effect of heavy casualties in a black division. In the event, the black soldiers died in large numbers when sent in to rescue the untrained white troops, trapped after entering the crater without ladders.

In August Grant had diagnosed the problem in the Shenandoah Valley as one of leadership and on August 1 sent Sheridan to take charge of Union forces. Sheridan's orders were simple – keep the crops in the Shenandoah out of Confederate hands, either through occupation of the farmlands, or destruction of the crops. Over the next three months, Sheridan systematically destroyed crops in the Shenandoah. Then, attacked by Early at Cedar Creek on October 19, Sheridan's army was

routed. Sheridan, absent when the battle began, rallied this broken army to decisively crush the apparently victorious Confederates with his counterattack.

In Georgia, Sherman and Johnston fought a war of maneuver from May through July. Johnston traded ground for time, hoping to keep Sherman from achieving a decisive victory prior to November's presidential election. Without a spectacular victory, it appeared that Lincoln would lose the election. His opponent, George McClellan running as a peace candidate, was viewed as likely to recognize Confederate independence.

Johnston's Fabian strategy was politically unpopular in the South and he was replaced by the more aggressive – and less able – John Hood on July 16. Given an opponent who was willing to fight stand-up battles, Sherman was able to use the military advantages he had. By July 20, Hood's army had been forced back to Atlanta. On September 2 – just in time to turn the political tide in Lincoln's favor, Sherman entered Atlanta.

Sherman soon realized holding Atlanta was impossible. His supply lines were untenable. He split his command in half, leaving Thomas to cover Tennessee from Hood's army, still in waiting in Alabama. Then Sherman evacuated Atlanta's civilians and destroyed its railroad and manufacturing industries. On November 15, he started his army marching through Georgia. His goal, unknown even to Grant, who had approved the operation, was Savannah.

Sherman arrived in Savannah on December 21, having cut a 60-mile swath through Georgia along the way. He destroyed everything of military importance within that strip – public buildings, railroads, and manufacturing facilities – seizing or destroying foodstuffs. Stragglers from both Confederate and Union armies added to the misery; stealing and destroying private property. Sherman's march demonstrated the impotence of the Confederate military and government, who were powerless to stop him. More demoralizing still for Confederate hopes was Lincoln's re-election, which made a negotiated end to the war impossible.

Meanwhile, Hood attempted to pressure the Union by invading Tennessee in a winter campaign. Thomas, deliberate in defense, had his command fall back slowly. Hood was badly beaten at Franklin, Tennessee, on November 30 by a smaller Union force, but pushed forward with the courage of desperation.

Realizing that Atlanta was untenable, and that holding it was unnecessary, Sherman abandoned the city, and then took his army to Savannah, Georgia. This "March to the Sea" demonstrated the hollowness of the Confederacy defense. (LOC)

His was the only Confederate army still on the offensive.

Thomas waited patiently for Hood at Nashville before striking. He was too patient for Grant, who sent Hooker to relieve him. Then, in a two-day battle on December 15 and 16, Thomas destroyed a Confederate army in a field battle. The survivors straggled back to the Carolinas, where they joined Joseph Johnston's army. Defeated, Hood resigned to be replaced by Johnston, the man he had relieved.

As Sherman marched his army north from Savannah through South Carolina and Tennessee, Grant and his army at Petersburg prevented Lee's army from intervening. Similarly Grant's troops blocked access as Sherman's army took Atlanta and marched through Georgia, and as Sheridan razed the Shenandoah. Because of these victories, the Confederate army grew steadily weaker as the Union campaigns reduced the food and supplies available to them.

By March, Lee knew the game was up. Grant was still pushing west, closer to the final railroad connecting Richmond to the South. Sherman's army, still in North Carolina, was closing on the Virginia border. Sheridan was back with Grant, having left behind a garrison in the Valley that Lee could not challenge without dangerously weakening Confederate forces at Petersburg. Lee's army was down to 50,000 men, facing 125,000 Union soldiers. On March 25, Lee decided to gamble. He assaulted the Union lines, intending to take Fort Stedman, key to the Union right.

In a way, Lee attempted to do to Grant what Grant had been attempting to do to Lee since the previous May – turn the enemy right flank, and roll up the army from behind. He was as unsuccessful as Grant had been. While Confederate troops reached Fort Stedman, and held it briefly, the Union

After initial Union disasters in the Shenandoah Valley, Grant sent Sheridan to command Union forces there. His judgment was vindicated when Sheridan rallied a routed Union army to decisively defeat Jubal Early at Winchester. (LOC)

Grant's headquarters at Spotsylvania

On May 8, 1864, Philip Sheridan (1), commanding the Cavalry Corps, got into an almighty row with his superior, Gen. George Meade (2), commanding the Army of the Potomac. Sheridan was Grant's most aggressive commander, and Meade – whose nickname was "Old Snapping Turtle" – was one of Grant's most pugnacious. Sheridan finished the argument by telling Meade, "I could whip Jeb Stuart – if only you would let me." Meade related the argument to Grant (3) who then replied, "Did he really say that? Well, he usually knows what he is talking about. Let him go ahead and do it." By nightfall, after a brief planning session shown here, Sheridan and cavalry rode out. The raid took the Cavalry Corps nearly to Richmond, and led to the battle of Yellow Tavern three days later, which resulted in the death of J. E. B. Stuart.

After a siege of nearly nine months, Grant finally flanked the Army of Northern Virginia at Five Forks. The Confederate defeat forced the evacuation of Petersburg and the Confederate capital of Richmond. (LOC)

counterattack pushed the Confederates back to their starting point. In terms of casualties, it was Cold Harbor in reverse.

Four days later, Grant's patience paid off. On April 1, Grant flanked Lee's right at Five Forks. Knowing this battle had drained the last of the Confederate reserves, and unwilling to let Lee's army slip away, Grant ordered a successful general assault on the Confederate lines on the morning of April 2. Petersburg and Richmond surrendered the following day. Lee succeeded in extricating his army, and began marching west to join Joe Johnston, who was then fighting Sherman in North Carolina.

Lee never got out of Virginia. Grant's goal was never Richmond, but rather Lee's Army. Grant pursued it with the same tenacity he had shown in pursuing every other objective he had gone after during the war. Richmond's occupation was almost incidental. Even before Petersburg fell, Grant sent out Sheridan's cavalry to cut off Lee's supplies. Again and again, during a week-long retreat, Lee's famished soldiers would arrive at a supply rendezvous to learn that the Yankees had been there first, and taken or destroyed the Confederate supplies.

Finally on May 9, Lee bowed to the inevitable. He responded positively to a letter sent by Grant inviting the army's surrender and promising generous terms. He agreed to meet Grant at a farmhouse near Appomattox, Virginia. Grant offered to release all members of the Army of Northern Virginia on parole until properly exchanged. While arms and public property was to be surrendered, officers were allowed to keep their sidearms and personal baggage and horses. The surrender included a clause that those surrendering were "not to be disturbed by the United States authorities so long as they observe their paroles, and the laws in force where they may reside." Grant further agreed to allow private soldiers to retain their horses, as they were individually owned.

The Civil War would drag on until June 19, when the final Confederate forces surrendered in Texas, but it effectively ended on April 9, 1865, with Lee's surrender at Appomattox.

OPPOSING COMMANDERS

Grant faced a number of different Confederate generals during the American Civil War. At Belmont, Henry, and Donelson, his primary opponent was Gideon Pillow. Following the fall of Fort Donelson, Grant was opposed by Albert Sidney Johnston until his death at Shiloh, whereupon command of Confederate forces fell to Pierre Beauregard. During Vicksburg, Grant's faced

John Pemberton. In Tennessee he fought forces led by Braxton Bragg. Finally, when Grant shifted to Virginia, he spent a year battling Robert E. Lee, perhaps the Confederacy's greatest general.

These men all had different strengths and weaknesses, yet one thing they shared was that Grant beat them all. Here is an evaluation of each man.

Gideon Pillow

Gideon Pillow was Grant's first major battlefield opponent, facing him at Belmont and Fort Donelson. Pillow was the model of the political general, exemplifying everything wrong with the breed. He was a law partner of James Polk, who was president 1845–49 during the Mexican–American War. On the strength of Pillow's service as a brigadier-general in the Tennessee militia, Polk appointed his friend a major-general in the United States Army during the Mexican War, and gave him command of a division in the American invasion force.

Pillow's service in that war, observed by Grant, was wretched. His attempts to claim credit for General Winfield Scott's victories at Contreras and Churubusco led to Pillow's court-martial, where he was exposed as the author of a mendacious and anonymous newspaper letter criticizing Scott. Only Polk's political intervention, as well as perjured testimony from a subordinate, saved Pillow from court martial. Despite his acquittal, he was discharged from the Army in 1848.

Pillow retained his commission in the Tennessee militia, and, by the start of the Civil War, was its senior major-general. On that basis, he received a commission as a brigadier-general in the Confederate States Army. His first task was to "liberate" Kentucky. Pillow's invasion of Kentucky, despite Confederate expectations, pushed then-neutral Kentucky into the Union camp. Later, as a subordinate of Leonidas Polk, he commanded a brigade at Columbus, Kentucky. Sent to occupy Belmont, he allowed his brigade to be surprised and routed by Grant's brigade. A counterattack launched by Leonidas Polk drove off the Yankees, so the battle was considered a Confederate victory. Pillow received the thanks of the Confederate Congress for his part in the battle.

Pillow was next given command of Fort Donelson in January 1862. His tenure as actual commander was brief, as when Donelson was reinforced, a more senior brigadier, John B. Floyd arrived. Floyd, another political general with no real military experience, deferred to Pillow giving him effective command. Pillow's performance was miserable. He remained inactive as Grant approached Donelson, allowing Grant to invest the fort unmolested. Then Pillow decided the fort was untenable. He attempted a breakout by assaulting the Union lines, which was initially successful. But Pillow paused the attack to resupply, and, by the time he resumed, Grant had reinforced his lines.

The Confederates were pushed back to Donelson. That night Floyd turned command over to Pillow and fled Donelson in a steamboat. Pillow, in his turn, delegated command to Buckner, and took off in a small boat,

Gideon Johnson Pillow. Following Donelson's surrender, Buckner asked Grant if he were disappointed in having allowed Pillow to escape. Grant replied that Pillow was of more use to the Union in command of Confederate forces than as a Union prisoner. (AC)

leaving Buckner to surrender the fort. Despite Pillow's pusillanimous behavior, he retained field commands until January 1863, when his behavior at Stones River led to his relief.

In many ways, Pillow was an excellent starter opponent for Grant. He gave Grant an opportunity to make mistakes against an opponent too incompetent to capitalize on them. Grant had known General Pillow in Mexico and knew he could run risks that would have been dangerous against other, more active commanders.

Albert Sidney Johnston

Albert Sidney Johnston commanded the Confederacy's Western Department in 1861 and early 1862, so, technically, he was Grant's opponent at Belmont, Fort Henry, and Fort Donelson, although he was not present at any of those battles. The only time he faced Grant in the field was at Shiloh, when he ambushed Grant's camp at Pittsburg Landing with the Army of Mississippi.

Born in Kentucky, Johnston attended West Point, graduating eighth in a class of 41 in 1826. He left the army in 1834, to care for his dying wife, moving to Texas after her death. During the Texas War of Independence, Johnston joined the revolutionary army as a private, but was quickly made an officer. By 1837 he was the senior brigadier-general in the Texas Republic's army. He left the Texas Army in 1843 to become a rancher.

Returning to military service when the Mexican–American War began, Johnston commanded the First Texas Rifle Volunteers regiment. He saw extensive action during that war, but returned to farming after its end. Zachary Taylor, as president, gave Johnston a major's commission in the United States Army in 1849. Johnston remained in the United States Army until the start of the Civil War, resigning his commission when Texas seceded. At that time he was a brigadier-general, and commanded the Army's Pacific Division.

California remained in the Union. Johnston joined a company of Confederate sympathizers in California, evaded arrest by state officials, and participated in a month-long horseback ride across the southwest deserts to reach Confederate territory. In September 1861, he was given a general's commission by Confederate President Jefferson Davis, with whom he had served in Mexico.

More than friendship justified Johnston's appointment. He had seen more combat in a command position than most Confederate generals. In addition to his service in both the Texas War of Independence and the Mexican–American War, Johnston had received promotion to brigadier-general as a result of a masterly performance in the Utah War of 1857–58. Johnston had resolved the dispute between Mormon settlers in Utah and the United States government through a combination of skilled diplomacy and implied force.

Johnston was put in command in the west on May 30, 1861, responsible for all Confederate forces west of the Appalachian Mountains. This included supervising the construction of the forts guarding the approaches to the South, and appointing the commanders of those forts, an area in which Johnston made bad choices. Johnston planned the attack on the Union position at Shiloh, and persisted in it, despite the opposition of his subordinates. He successfully surprised the Union army there, and almost succeeded in pushing his foes into the Tennessee River.

Of all Grant's opponents, Johnston was the commander most similar to him. Both shared the ability to master the battlefield when in battle. The strategic weaknesses Johnston showed were similar to those exhibited by Grant over the same period. Experience would have cured Johnston's weaknesses as it did for Grant. Whether Johnston would have been Grant's equal or even greater than Grant as a general will forever remain unanswered.

Albert Sidney Johnston. At the time of his death at Shiloh, Johnston was considered the Confederacy's best general. His wound should not have been fatal, but nerve damage from an 1840s duel in Texas left Johnston unaware of the seriousness of his injury. (AC)

John C. Pemberton

John C. Pemberton faced Grant during the Vicksburg campaign, and eventually lost the city to him. Despite fighting for the Confederacy, Pemberton was born and raised in Philadelphia, Pennsylvania, one of a handful of northern-born professional Army officers to choose the Confederacy. Two of his brothers served in the Union Army during the Civil War.

Pemberton attended the United States Military Academy, and remained in the Army upon graduation in 1837 until he resigned his commission in 1861 when the Civil War broke out. Like Grant, Pemberton was firmly in the middle of his class, graduating 27th out of a class of 50. Pemberton was commissioned in the artillery, and served much of his United States Army career in the 4th Artillery.

Pemberton saw combat in the First Seminole War (1837–38), the Mexican–American War, Second Seminole War (1849–50), Third Seminole War (1856–57), and participated in the Utah War. During the Mexican–American War he was present at most of the major battles in that war, where he distinguished himself. He received a brevet promotion to captain for gallant conduct at Monterrey and a brevet promotion to major at Molino del Rey. He was wounded at the battle for Mexico City.

Following the Mexican–American War he remained in the Army. Over the period from 1849 through 1861, most of his service was in the South, particularly Florida. This included serving in the Second and Third Seminole Wars. He also married a woman from Virginia. When the Southern states seceded, Pemberton opted to "Go South," tendering his resignation from the United States Army and accepting a commission as a lieutenant-colonel in the Confederate States Army, defending his adopted state of Virginia.

His professional competence and knowledge of artillery meant that Pemberton was a brigadier-general by June 1861 and a major-general by January 1862. But his abrasive personality and northern origins made him unpopular. While commanding the Confederate Department of South Carolina and Georgia in 1862, the governors of both states mistrusted Pemberton so much that they petitioned for him to be removed. There was an opening in Mississippi, following Stirling Price's defeat at Holly Springs, so

John Pemberton. Born in Pennsylvania, but tied to the South through ties of marriage and years of living in the South, Pemberton was never fully trusted by other Southerners. Fear of an adverse reaction to abandoning Vicksburg was one reason why Pemberton chose to remain there in an untenable position. (USAHI)

in October 1862 Pemberton was promoted to lieutenant-general and reassigned to Mississippi. His primary task was holding Vicksburg.

Pemberton's defense of Vicksburg was initially successful. He restored the morale of the Army of Mississippi, and established a set of fortifications that stymied Grant's attempts to take Vicksburg from either the north or east. Yet Pemberton placed too much importance on positional defense. Grant's swing south of Vicksburg, especially once Grant moved independently of his own supply lines, caught Pemberton flat-footed. Flanked by Grant, Pemberton soon retreated back into Vicksburg. Fearing condemnation if he abandoned Vicksburg because of his northern origins, Pemberton chose to make a stand in the city. Instead of losing Vicksburg, Pemberton lost both Vicksburg and his army, the largest field force in Mississippi.

Released on parole after Vicksburg, Pemberton remain unemployed until May 1864, when he returned to artillery, which he commanded at Richmond in 1865. After the war he resumed farming in Virginia, and late in life he returned to Pennsylvania, where he died and was buried.

Braxton Bragg

Braxton Bragg faced Grant as one of the Confederate corps commanders at Shiloh, and also as commander of the Army of Tennessee during the siege of Chattanooga. He was Grant's most controversial opponent, capable of creating strong reactions in both critics and defenders.

Born in Warrenton, North Carolina, in 1817, Bragg attended West Point at age 16. He graduated in the 1837 class that included John Pemberton, with Bragg fifth in a class of 50. Opting for artillery upon being commissioned, he saw service, but not combat, with the 3rd Artillery in the Second Seminole War in 1840.

Bragg gained a reputation as an argumentative officer and a rigid disciplinarian in the years prior to the Mexican–American War. After publishing a series of articles criticizing Winfield Scott, Bragg was charged with and convicted of disobedience to orders and disrespect towards superior officers. He received a reprimand and was suspended for two months.

He redeemed his professional reputation in the Army with his performance during the Mexican–American War, providing artillery support critical to the American victory at Buena Vista. While the battle made him a hero in the United States, and he was professionally admired by peers and superiors, he was personally disliked due to his abrasive personality. At one point, a disgruntled soldier rolled a lit artillery shell under Bragg's cot, while Bragg was sleeping. Although his cot was destroyed, Bragg was unhurt.

Bragg left the Army in 1855, having married a wealthy sugar heiress from Louisiana in 1849. He purchased a sugar plantation in Louisiana, which he ran with the same efficiency as his artillery units, making a profit almost immediately. He adopted Louisiana as his home, taking a colonel's commission in the Louisiana militia.

While supporting slavery, he strongly opposed secession. Regardless, when Louisiana seceded, he remained loyal to his adopted state and accepted a commission in the Confederate Army. By September 1861 he was a major-general with a reputation of producing trained and disciplined soldiers. He served as a corps commander at Shiloh, and also as Johnston's chief of staff at that battle. Bragg was the man most responsible for attacking rather than bypassing the Hornet's Nest, which allowed Grant to reconstitute Union lines.

Following Shiloh, Bragg, promoted to general, began a summer offensive to take Kentucky from central Tennessee. Despite initial successes, the campaign fell apart due to poor coordination between the armies and Bragg's own vacillations. The campaign culminated in the battle of Stones River, a bloody draw that forced a Confederate retreat to central Tennessee. It also led to mutual recriminations between Bragg and his subordinate generals.

In 1863, Bragg was pushed out of Tennessee into northern Georgia, losing Chattanooga, Tennessee, a critical railroad junction. In September 1863, significantly reinforced, Bragg attacked the Union Army at Chickamauga, forcing a Yankee retreat to Chattanooga. Bragg besieged Chattanooga, not completely surrounding it, but leaving a few rugged and easily raided mountain roads as the only way to get supplies to the town. Grant defeated him, in part because he weakened his forces because of personality conflicts with subordinates – he sent away Longstreet's corps at a critical point, for example.

Relieved after Chattanooga, Bragg served in Richmond for much of the remainder of the war, quarreling with everyone. He lost his home after the war, but became a civil engineer, working on both river and harbor projects.

Braxton Bragg. In his memoirs Grant would credit the Union victory at Chattanooga as having been made easier by Bragg's mistakes. Among them, Grant cited sending away his ablest corps commander with 20,000 troops, sending away a division of troops immediately before the battle, and misplacing his troops at Chattanooga. (AC)

Robert E. Lee

Grant's opponent in Virginia in 1864–65, Robert E. Lee commanded the Army of Northern Virginia between 1862 and 1865 and is considered the greatest Confederate general of the Civil War. Born in Virginia in 1807, Lee was the son of Harry "Light Horse" Lee, a Revolutionary War hero, imprisoned for debt when Robert E. Lee was an infant. His father's fame and disgrace drove Lee throughout his life.

Lee graduated from West Point in 1829, second in a class of 46. He was commissioned in the engineers, which was considered the most prestigious branch of the United States Army. He established a reputation for professional excellence as an engineer over the next 15 years. He supervised the construction of fortifications, improved navigation on the inland rivers and helped survey the border between Michigan and Ohio. In 1831 he married Mary Custis, a great-granddaughter of Martha Washington.

Lee participated in the Mexican–American War, distinguishing himself while serving as an aide to Winfield Scott. A reconnaissance Lee conducted was instrumental to the American victory, allowing Scott's army to follow a route considered impassable. He was brevetted twice for bravery, ending the war as a brevet lieutenant-colonel. He met Grant during that war, a meeting the two recalled during their negotiations at Appomattox. While Lee remembered the meeting, he did not recall Grant's appearance.

Grant respected Robert E. Lee, but did not believe him to be invincible, telling his subordinates, "Some of you always seem to think he is suddenly going to turn a double somersault, and land in our rear and on both of our flanks at the same time. Go back to your command, and try to think what we are going to do ourselves, instead of what Lee is going to do." (USAHI)

After the Mexican–American War, Lee was marked for promotion and was viewed by someone capable of eventually commanding the United States Army. He served as superintendent of the United States Military Academy, and as lieutenant-colonel of the 2nd Cavalry Regiment in Texas. In Washington when John Brown seized the federal arsenal at Harpers Ferry in 1859, Lee commanded the force that recaptured the arsenal.

When Texas seceded Lee was in Texas. He returned to his estate at Arlington, Virginia. Lee viewed secession as rebellion, yet he regarded his allegiance to Virginia as greater than his allegiance to the United States. Lee turned down a major-general's commission in the United States Army to fight in defense of his native Virginia.

Despite his formidable post-Civil War military reputation, Lee's war started haltingly. He was defeated at the battle of Cheat Mountain in West Virginia. Then, while commanding the Department of South Carolina, Georgia, and Florida, he directed the defense of Savannah, Georgia, when Fort Pulaski was captured by a Union expedition. Thereafter, he was appointed military advisor to Jefferson Davis, President of the Confederacy. Lee was derided as "Granny Lee" and "the King of Spades" for insisting on heavy entrenchment around Richmond.

Lee's career revived in June 1862 after he replaced the injured Joe Johnston as commander of the Army of Northern Virginia during McClellan's Peninsular Campaign in 1862. With the Army of the Potomac at the gates of Richmond, Lee launched a counteroffensive. In a series of encounters known as the Seven Days' Battle, Lee pushed the Union Army back to its base on the James River. Lee would bedevil the Army of the Potomac for the next 13 months, before experiencing a substantive defeat at Gettysburg, Pennsylvania. Even after that, the Union did not seriously challenge the Army of Northern Virginia, until May 1864 when Grant started his Overland Campaign.

Supporters of both continue to debate whether Lee or Grant was the superior commander. Yet Grant has to be given the edge based on three factors. While Lee managed to outmaneuver Grant during the 1864 Overland Campaign, much of the reason for Lee's success lay in the nature of their armies. Lee's was the best that the Confederacy had. Grant's was inferior to the troops that Grant had developed in the West. Had Grant faced Lee with the swift-moving Army of the Tennessee instead of the sluggish Army of the Potomac, Grant would likely have outmarched Lee and defeated his army in 1864.

Grant was also Lee's superior in grand strategy. Grant conceived a plan that successfully defeated the Confederacy – not in one theater, but over the United States. Lee was focused on defending Virginia to the exclusion of other factors. Winning the Civil War for the Confederacy was the best way of defending Virginia, not fighting an essentially defensive role in northern Virginia.

Finally, however inelegantly, Grant defeated Lee: Grant won. He developed a theater-level strategy that Lee was unable to counter. Nor was it inevitable that any general other than Grant could have succeeded in doing this. McClellan and Meade had failed to do so, even when given greater superiority over Lee than Grant often enjoyed.

INSIDE THE MIND

If asked to describe Grant, most people today would state three things: he was a drunk, he was a military butcher, and he was an implacable enemy of the Confederacy – "Unconditional Surrender" Grant. All three popular views misrepresent basic aspects of Grant's character.

Grant had problems with alcohol. He was unusually susceptible to the effects of alcohol, and one drink would have the effect of three or four on an average adult. He was also often a spree drinker, unable to stop once he started. Yet he was not a typical drunk. He drank only when separated from his wife for long periods. Even then he drank only when desperately unhappy or under extreme stress. His drinking in California followed this pattern. Yet outside the army prior to the Civil War Grant did not drink to excess. "Useless" Grant was never the town drunk, despite failures at business. Certainly he was not drinking during the period when Halleck was trying to have him removed or in the period before Shiloh.

This is not to say Grant never drank. The frustrations of the Vicksburg Campaign took an emotional toll on Grant. At two points – once in mid-April when the planning for the spring campaign had been completed, and once in June, shortly after the battle of Milliken's Bend – Grant went off on multiday benders. He went on a similar spree after the failed assault at Cold Harbor.

Yet after each binge Grant sobered up and returned to duty. More importantly, his staff covered for Grant. This included Charles Anderson Dana, a journalist sent by Washington to monitor Grant's behavior. Dana was present at the first incident, when a report by him would have led to Grant's relief. Dana kept quiet, believing that neither McClernand nor any of Grant's corps commanders would be likely to have seen the Vicksburg campaign to a successful conclusion.

Grant's reputation as a butcher is also overstated. Grant commanded at several of the bloodiest battles fought by the Union in the Civil War. Yet he disliked making frontal assaults on fortified positions. He preferred maneuver and flank attacks, although he would order an assault – as at Donelson – if he felt conditions warranted it. Many of the most disastrous frontal assaults at Grant's battles – such as that at Cold Harbor and the battle of the Crater at Petersburg – resulted from subordinate commanders making ill-advised or badly planned assaults.

Grant's anchor throughout his life, especially during the Civil War, was his family. When Grant began yielding to drink, his staff realized the best cure would be the presence of Julia and the children. Grant kept them with him whenever possible. (AC)

At other times, including one of the assaults at Vicksburg, Grant was misled by over-optimistic or misleading reports from subordinates. Given an erroneous report by McClernand that he had achieved a breakthrough, Grant ordered his other corps commanders to attack. In reality, the attack had failed, and the additional assaults simply yielded more casualties, for which Grant – not McClernand – was blamed.

Grant was implacably opposed to secession and personally disliked slavery. He freed the one slave he owned, an unwanted gift, despite the considerable financial loss manumission entailed. Yet he tolerated the institution prior to and during the early years of the Civil War as the price of maintaining the Union. Once secession occurred, Grant fought to maintain the Union.

This desire contributed to his willingness to take the battle to the enemy. It was Grant's belief that the quickest way to win the war was to destroy the Confederate armies, and that the only way to do that was through battle. His early battles in Missouri and Tennessee also showed him that the enemy was as worried about him as he was about them.

Yet it would be overstating Grant's antipathy to slavery and secession to claim that either made him unwilling to accept surrender on terms other than unconditional surrender. Grant was always willing to use conditional surrender when it served his greater goal of re-achieving unity. When the Confederate garrison of Vicksburg surrendered, he permitted one condition, and released the garrison on parole. Many in Washington criticized this because they believed that the paroled soldiers would return to the battlefield before being properly exchanged. Grant realized that risk was more than balanced by the demoralizing effect that the returning, dispirited garrison members would exert on their neighbors.

Similar thinking can be seen behind the terms Grant offered Lee at Appomattox. So long as individual Confederates observed the terms of parole until exchanged, the Federal Government could not prosecute them for their actions during the war. They could never be "properly exchanged," as the legal agent for their exchange, the Confederate government, no longer existed, so it was effectively a lifetime amnesty for those that went home to peaceful lives. When Lee informed Grant that many of the horses used by Confederate cavalrymen and artillerymen were their private property, and that they would need them for spring planting, Grant ordered his officers to allow private soldiers to keep their personal mounts. Once the surrender was signed, Grant asked if Lee's men needed rations. They did of course, so Grant turned over 25,000 rations to his former foes.

It was a remarkably generous settlement, and put an end to the nickname "Unconditional Surrender" Grant. Grant had fought a hard war, imposing hard terms during the hostilities in order to win as quickly as possible. Now he gave generous terms in order to win the peace. With his signature on the surrender instrument, he forestalled the capacity of Congress to seek vengeance. Congress was unhappy about this infringement, but they were unwilling to buck the popular Grant.

He also encouraged other Confederate forces to yield to the same generous terms, forestalling guerrilla resistance to the Federal government. It was one thing to take to the hills and fight to the death as a proscribed rebel, facing imprisonment or execution. It was an entirely different thing if you were given legal amnesty so long as you behaved and lived your life as you had previously.

WHEN WAR IS DONE

At the Civil War's end Grant had achieved his life's ambitions, although they were probably more modest than most people imagine. He was a success at his career, for virtually the first time in his life. True, Grant had imagined being a successful professor or farmer rather than a successful soldier. And while he disliked war, he found that he enjoyed the military life, especially from a position at the top of the command structure. Further, he was financially secure. His Army pay was substantial, and even his pension, once he retired, guaranteed a comfortable lifestyle.

He chose to remain in the Army as its senior general. Congress promoted Grant to full general in 1866, the first officer to hold four-star rank in American history. As its senior general Grant directed the Army as second-in-command to President Andrew Johnson, who had inherited the office after Lincoln was assassinated in April 1865, a few weeks before Appomattox.

The two men clashed almost immediately. Johnson, a Tennessee Democrat who stayed loyal to the Union, wanted to prosecute Confederate officers who had previously served in the United States Army for treason. Grant refused to authorize such trials, as they were contrary to the terms negotiated at Appomattox and other subsequent surrenders. Johnson persisted until Grant threatened resignation. As this would have led to the collapse of Johnson's presidency, Johnson backed down.

A second flash point emerged over civil rights. Johnson, a southerner, opposed equal rights for blacks, and refused to enforce civil rights laws passed by Congress over the presidential veto. Grant had been willing to tolerate slavery prior to the Civil War and did not favor emancipation during the early years of it. Yet he disliked slavery. He viewed abolition as the harvest the South had reaped through their resistance, especially since nearly 200,000 blacks, mostly slaves, had fought for the Union. Grant had the Army enforce civil rights laws, an action Johnson could not prevent, as Grant was enforcing existing law.

The result was inevitable. Grant, a Stephen Douglas Democrat prior to the Civil War, aligned himself with the Radical Republicans, the party's extreme abolitionist wing, who favored a harsh reconstruction. He accepted the Republican nomination for president in 1868. Still the most popular man in the nation, he won the election based largely on support from Northern veterans and black freedmen in the South.

Grant became the first full general in the United States Army, but he did not receive this promotion until a year after the Civil War ended, in 1866. He was a major-general through most of the war, and a lieutenant-general only during its last year. (LOC)

As president, Grant found that he could not transfer his competence as a general to a civilian political office. While Grant was personally honest, many of his cabinet appointments were not. Nor were many in Congress scrupulously honest, including some in the Republican majority – and Grant frequently deferred to that institution. The result was an administration tainted by financial scandal and corruption. Additionally, Grant's efforts to establish equal rights for blacks faltered, with a Southern backlash to the harsh reconstruction policies insisted upon by the Radical Republicans. While Grant was re-elected in 1872 – by a narrower margin than his 1868 race – his presidency was largely a failure.

His plunge into politics also weakened Grant financially. The presidency was a civilian office. To run, he had to forfeit his Army salary and pension. While his presidential salary was larger than his general's salary, as president Grant had to entertain at his own expense on a lavish scale. Once he left office in March 1877, that salary stopped, and there were then no presidential pensions.

He left office at a low point of popularity. His actions during the financial Panic of 1873 had been heavily criticized, and he had also been tarred with the backlash of the Whiskey Ring Scandal. Federal officials, many of them political appointees, had been caught siphoning off excise tax monies on alcohol into their own pockets. Grant decided to take a vacation. He left the United States for a world tour with Julia.

It lasted over two years. He went where he wanted to go, was feted by world leaders, including Queen Victoria, Otto von Bismarck, Pope Leo XIII, and Emperor Meiji and Empress Shoken of Japan. He dabbled in diplomacy, attempting to negotiate a settlement between Japan and China over the Ryukyu Islands. He returned to the United States in September 1879, thinner and happier. The trip depleted his savings, however.

He attempted to secure the Republican presidential nomination in 1880, seeking a third term as president. His efforts failed, but Grant supported the eventual Republican nominee, James Garfield, who scraped a narrow victory.

To restore his fortunes, Grant had gone into partnership with Ferdinand Ward, investing $100,000 (virtually all he owned) into the partnership. As usual when dealing with financial matters, Grant picked the wrong partner. Ward's investment plan was a Ponzi scheme. By the time it collapsed in 1884, Grant, the mark in Ward's game, was a further $500,000 in debt.

To compound Grant's woes, he developed esophageal cancer in 1884, the result of thousands of cigars smoked since Donelson. By the time it was diagnosed in February 1885, it was incurable and he only had months to live. His major concern was providing for Julia. In 1884 he was living on the charity of friends, with creditors ready to swoop down and seize any new income he received. But at that late stage of his life he discovered he had one more talent. He was an engaging author. In 1884 *Century Magazine* had asked Grant to write four articles about his Civil War experiences. Offered $500 per article, Grant accepted.

Mark Twain, who had befriended Grant earlier, convinced Grant to write his Civil War memoirs. Twain owned a publishing house and offered Grant a lavish royalty – which could be assigned to Julia, so as to keep it away from Grant's creditors. Grant then began his last campaign – to finish his memoirs before his death.

He finished the book days before he died. It was one of the best military memoirs written. By then, advance sales of 150,000 copies had already been made, assuring that the book would be a financial success. To many it seemed that the will to complete the book alone had sustained Grant in his final months. Having delivered the manuscript, Grant's final victory had been secured. He died July 23, 1885, surrounded by his wife and children.

A LIFE IN WORDS

Ulysses Grant may have had more words written about him by contemporaries than any general in United States history since George Washington. Some of those words attempted to filch credit for Grant's battlefield successes. Certainly superiors such as John C. Frémont and Henry Halleck, as well as subordinates like John McClernand, were never shy about claiming that Grant's success was due to their genius. These claims were belied by their performance in the absence of Grant, or more accurately when Grant was not in charge on their battlefields.

Grant finally caught the presidential grub after the war's end. He would serve two terms as president, and try unsuccessfully for a third. This is a picture of his second inauguration in 1872. (LOC)

Ulysses Grant surrounded by his family in July 1885. Taken only a few days before his death from throat cancer, it was one of the last photographs taken of him. (AC)

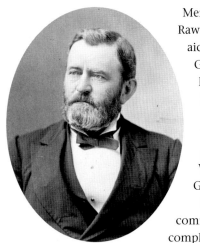

Ulysses S. Grant while President of the United States. Gone is the slim general of the Civil War, and the clarity of purpose that he possessed during the hostilities. (LOC)

Members of his staff also claimed credit for Grant's military genius. John Rawlins, a Galena lawyer and acquaintance of Grant who served as his aide-de-camp and chief of staff felt that he was the mastermind behind Grant's victories. Rawlins was little more than a glorified clerk with no knowledge of the military before serving with Grant. Yet James H. Wilson and Sylvanus Cadwallader, two other minor members of Grant's staff, supported Rawlins' assertions. Following Grant's death, Wilson claimed that Grant was a timid commander who had to be guided by Rawlins and himself. The claims reveal far more about Wilson's and Cadwallader's feeling for Rawlins and antipathy towards Grant than they do about history.

Others viewed Grant more favorably, particularly Grant's ultimate commander, Abraham Lincoln. While the tale that Lincoln told a complaining Halleck to "Find out what Grant drinks, and send my other commanders a case," is probably apocryphal, Lincoln's admiration was clear in other statements. When asked about Grant in July 1863 Lincoln told General Daniel Sickles "I kind of like U. S. Grant. He doesn't worry and bother me. He isn't shrieking for reinforcements all the time. He takes the troops we can safely give him… and does the best he can, and he doesn't grumble and scold all the while."

Lincoln made those comments before meeting Grant. After meeting him for the first time Lincoln stated, "Well, I hardly know what to think of him. He's the quietest little fellow you ever saw. He makes the least fuss of any man you ever knew. I believe two or three times he has been in this room a minute or so before I knew he was here. It's about so all around. The only evidence you have that he's in any place is that he makes things git! Wherever he is, things move."

Lincoln was not the only one impressed with Grant. When a civilian in Savannah, Georgia criticized Grant shortly after Sherman's army arrived, William Tecumseh Sherman told the man, "General Grant is a great general. I know him well. He stood by me when I was crazy, and I stood by him when he was drunk; and now, sir, we stand by each other always."

While Sherman claimed to know Grant well, and admired him as a friend, he never claimed to understand Grant. In an 1879 letter, written when he was commander of the United States Army, Sherman stated, "I knew him as a cadet at West Point, as a lieutenant of the Fourth Infantry, as a

Abraham Lincoln's letter to Grant at the start of the Overland Campaign of 1864. Written on April 30, 1864, it expresses Lincoln's confidence in Grant. (AC)

citizen of St Louis, and as a growing general all through the bloody Civil War. Yet to me he is a mystery, and I believe he is a mystery to himself."

Others noticed Grant's work ethic. In a letter sent to Secretary of War Edward Staunton on December 14, 1863, General David Hunter wrote of Grant, "He is a hard worker, who writes his own dispatches and orders and does his own thinking. He is modest, quiet, never swears, and seldom drinks.... He listens quietly to the opinions of others and then judges promptly for himself; and he is prompt to avail himself of all the errors of his enemy. He is certainly a good judge of men, and has called around him valuable counselors."

Grant even gained the admiration of his foes. During the Civil War Lee wrote to his son Custis with some asperity of Grant,

"His talent and strategy consists in accumulating overwhelming numbers." Yet in late 1865, when someone spoke harshly of Grant while Lee was at Washington University (later Washington and Lee) Lee responded "Sir, if you ever again presume to speak disrespectfully of General Grant in my presence, either you or I will sever his connection with this university."

General John B. Gordon, CSA, wrote of Grant in his memoirs:

Despite Grant's failings as president and in business after leaving the presidency, he remained a beloved figure. Grant's tomb was funded by private donations, and built on a monumental scale. Grant and his wife rest there in a mausoleum. (AC)

General Grant was not endowed by nature with the impressive personality and soldierly bearing of Winfield Scott Hancock, nor with the peculiarly winning and magnetic presence of William McKinley... but under a less attractive exterior he combined the strong qualities of both.... General Grant's truly great qualities—his innate modesty, his freedom from every trace of vain-glory or ostentation, his magnanimity in victory, his genuine sympathy for his brave and sensitive foemen, and his inflexible resolve to protect paroled Confederates against any assault, and vindicate, at whatever cost, the sanctity of his pledge to the vanquished—will give him a place in history no less renowned and more to be envied than that secured by his triumphs as a soldier or his honors as a civilian.

Perhaps no greater tribute could be paid.

FURTHER READING

It is hard to make suggestions as to further reading on Ulysses Grant's military career, because so many excellent and readable accounts exist. It seems unfair to single one out while ignoring others.

The place to start is with Grant's own words. The four articles he wrote for *Century Magazine* were reprinted in *Battles & Leaders of the Civil War*, listed in the bibliography. It is still in print and available online. Grant's *Personal Memoirs of U.S. Grant* (also listed below) is also widely available, including online at Project Gutenberg (http://www.gutenberg.org/). Grant writes in a clear and engaging style which is readable as well as informative. Grant's writings tend to be shaded in Grant's favor (he glossed over why he left the Army in 1854, for example), but are still worthwhile.

Other period memoirs are also worth reading, particularly Sherman's. William T. Sherman was as talented a writer as he was a general. Others, especially those written by Sylvanus Cadwallader and James Wilson are more problematic. Some of their claims are historical fiction rather than history.

For those seeking later works J. F. C. Fuller's *The Generalship of Ulysses S. Grant* (Dodd, Mead and Company: New York, 1929), and Bruce Catton's *U.S. Grant and the American Military Tradition* (Little, Brown: Boston, 1954) remain readable, if dated.

Grant is an evergreen subject for authors, with nearly 100 books on Grant having been written over the last 50 years. The books listed below are not a complete list of my sources, but represent either major ones or books that should be accessible due to recent publication.

Dugard, Martin, *The Training Ground: Grant, Lee, Sherman, and Davis in the Mexican War, 1846–1848*, Little, Brown and Co.: New York, 2008

Flood, Charles Bracelen, *Grant and Sherman: The Friendship That Won the Civil War*, Farrar, Straus and Giroux: New York, 2005

Grant, Ulysses S., *Personal Memoirs of U.S. Grant*, Charles Webster: New York, 1885

Johnson, Robert Underwood, and Buel, Clarence Clough, *Battles and Leaders of the Civil War*, The Century Company: New York, 1887–88

Perret, Geoffrey, *Ulysses S. Grant: Soldier and President*, Random House: New York, 1997

Porter, Horace, *Campaigning with Grant*, Putnam: New York, 1897

Sherman, William T., *The Memoirs of General W. T. Sherman*, D. Appleton & Company: New York, 1889

Simon, John Y., ed., *The Papers of Ulysses S. Grant* (8 Volumes), Southern Illinois University Press: Carbondale, 1967

Simpson, Brooks D., *Ulysses S. Grant: Triumph Over Adversity, 1822–1865*, Houghton Mifflin: New York, 2000

US War Dept., *The War of the Rebellion: A Compilation of the Official Records of the Union and Confederate Armies* (128 volumes), Washington, DC: GPO, 1880–1901

GLOSSARY

Brevet Promotion or Rank – a temporary rank awarded to give an officer extra authority or to reward bravery. An officer with a brevet rank outranked those with a permanent rank below him. If two officers had the same brevet rank, but different permanent rank, the officer with the higher permanent rank was the superior officer.

Exchange – a formal process to trade prisoners between two sets of combatants. Each combatant would create a commission to oversee the exchange process, and keep records of who was exchanged. Exchanged prisoners could return to combat.

Flag Officer – a United States Navy rank established by Congress in 1857 corresponding to that of commodore. It was superseded by the rank of rear admiral in 1862.

Parole – an agreement to release a prisoner of war who agrees not to return to combat until formally exchanged for a prisoner of war captured by his own side. A prisoner who violated parole (escaped or returned to combat before being exchanged) was considered an illegal combatant and could legally be shot.

Permanent Rank – the permanent rank held by an officer based on his commission issued by the United States Congress. It is lower than temporary or brevet rank held during wartime, and is the rank to which the officer reverts in peacetime.

Regular Army/Regular Commission – the Regular Army was the national army of the United States. Those officers granted commissions in the Regular Army held regular commissions. An officer with a Regular Army commission outranked all officers of the same or lower volunteer rank.

Volunteer Rank – a rank issued by a state or (for ranks higher than colonel) by the Congress to those in state or militia organizations. Officers could hold both regular and volunteer commissions. Although the regular rank outranked an equivalent volunteer rank, officers usually held volunteer ranks higher than their regular rank. For a while Grant held the regular rank of brigadier-general while he was a volunteer major-general. (A major-general – volunteer or regular – outranked a regular brigadier-general.)

INDEX